A Manual of the Antiquity of Man

by J. P. MacLean

PREFACE.

In lecturing upon the Antiquity of Man I have found the minds of the people prepared to receive the evidences, and ready to believe the conclusions of the geologists. I have felt the need of a popular work to place in the hands of the public, that would be both instructive and welcome. The works of Lyell and Lubbock are too elaborate and too expensive to meet the popular need. My object has been to give an outline of the subject sufficient to afford a reasonable acquaintance with the facts connected with the new science, to such as desire the information but cannot pursue it further, and to serve as a manual for those who intend to become more proficient.

As the Unity of Language and the Unity of the Race are so closely connected with the subject, I have added the two chapters on these questions, hoping they will be acceptable to the reader. It was my intention to have written a more extended chapter on the relation of the Holy Scriptures to this subject, but was forced to condense, as I had done in other chapters, in order not to transcend the proposed limits of the book.

In the preparation of this work I have freely used Lyell's "Antiquity of Man" and "Principles of Geology," Lubbock's "Pre-Historic Times," Buchner's "Man in the Past, Present, and Future," Figuier's "Primitive Man," Wilson's "Pre-Historic Man," Keller's "Lake-Dwellings," the works of Charles Darwin, Dana's "Manual of Geology," Huxley's "Man's Place in Nature," Prichard's "Natural History of Man," Pouchet's "Plurality of the Human Race," and others, referred to in the margins.

I am indebted to my friend, Mr. Frank Cushing, for the ideal restoration of the Neanderthal Man. The engraving was made especially for this work. The references to Buchner are from his work entitled, "Man in the Past, Present and Future."

CONTENTS.

CHAPTER I.

INTRODUCTION. PAGE Interest in the subject--Influence of Lyell--Usher's Chronology--Aime Boue first to proclaim the high antiquity of man--Dr. Schmerling the founder--Boucher de Perthes the apostle--Classifications by Lubbock, Lartet, Renevier, and Westropp--Plan of the work--No Universal Age of Stone, Bronze, or Iron--Epochs not sharply defined--Outlines of History-- Superstitious Notions--Skull from Constatt--Stone hatchet from London-- Cavern of Gailenreuth--Axes from Hoxne--Human jaw from Maestricht-- Skeleton from Lahr-- "Reliquiae Diluvianae"--Discoveries by Tournal and Christol-- Engis and Enghihoul Caverns--Schmerling's labors--Lyell's opinions-- Arrow mark on skull of Cave-Bear--Boucher de Perthes and the Valley of the Somme--Jaw of Moulin-Quignon-- Kent's Hole--Fossil Man of Denise--Remains from the Manzanares--Cave of Aurignac--Lyell declares his belief-- Lake- Dwellings of Switzerland Neanderthal Skull--Caverns near Torquay--Cave of Massat--Cave of Lourdes--Caverns of Ariege--Tertiary at St. Prest--Implements near Gosport-- Bones from Colmar--Implements near Bournemouth--Trou de la Naulette--Bones near Savonia--Reindeer Station--Foreland Cliff--Fossil Man of Mentone--Other Discoveries near Mentone.

CHAPTER II.

GLACIAL EPOCH.

Starting point for the investigation--Advance of the ice-- Fauna of Europe-- Geological Period--Probable Date--Probable Duration--Evidences of the Existence of Man--Implements from Hampshire--Flint tools at Bournemouth-- Oval flint from Foreland Cliff--Implements from the Valley of the Somme-- Jaw of Moulin-Quignon--Implements from the Seine--Axes near Madrid-- Kent's Hole--Brixham Cave--Human jaw from Maestricht--Skeleton from Lahr- -Cave of La Naulette-- Implements from Hoxne--Bones from Colmar.

CHAPTER III.

GLACIAL--CONTINUED.

Belgian Caverns--Caverns of Liege--Engis Skull--Remarks of Prof. Huxley--Views of Busk, Schmerling, Buchner, and Vogt-- Neanderthal Skull--Prof. Huxley, Dr. Buchner, and Dr. Fuhlrott on Geological time of Neanderthal Skull--Opinions of Huxley, Buchner, Schaaffhausen, and Busk--Skull from the Loess of the Rhine, Constatt, Cochrane's Cave, Island of Moen, Minsk, and Plau--Borreby Skulls--Human skulls of Arno.

CHAPTER IV.

PRE-GLACIAL EPOCHS.

North America during the Tertiary--Europe--Climate--Fauna of Eocene--Of Miocene--Of Pliocene--Traces of Man--Opinions of Lyell, Lubbock, and A. R. Wallace--Man in the Pliocene-- Hearth under Osars--Human bones from Savonia--Discoveries at St. Prest--Skull from Altaville--Prof. Denton's Statement-- Man in the Miocene--Flints from Pontlevoy--Flint-flake from Aurillac--Marks on bones near Pouance--Implements from Colorado and Wyoming--Eocene--Glacial Periods during the Miocene.

CHAPTER V.

CONDITION OF MAN IN THE EARLIEST TIMES.

No knowledge of the first appearance of Man--Fauna of India during the Miocene--Intellect of Man--Contests with the Beasts--A weapon invented--Earliest type--Advancement slow-- Climate changes--Sufferings of Man--Known by the Remains-- Structure of the Neanderthal Man--Engis Man--Men both large and small--Animal structure of jaws from La Naulette and Moulin-Quignon. 63

CHAPTER VI.

INTER-GLACIAL EPOCH.

Condition of the earth--Numerous traces of Man--Cave of Aurignac--Conclusions of Lartet and Cartailhac--Caverns of Maccagnone--Wokey Hole--Fossil Man of Denise--Reindeer Station on the Schusse--Dr. Buchner's Conclusions.

CHAPTER VII.

CONDITION OF MAN IN THE INTER-GLACIAL.

Length of the Inter-Glacial--Man an improvable being-- Implements improved--Art of engraving begun--Religious nature--Denton's description of primeval man--Language improved.

CHAPTER VIII.

REINDEER EPOCH.

Advance of the Glaciers--Fauna---Reindeer epoch a distinct one--Evidences of the existence of Man--Caves of Central and Southern France--Implements from Les Eyzies--Relics from La Madeleine--Workshops of Laugerie-Haute and Laugerie-Basse-- Cave and rock shelters of Bruniquel--Cave of Gourdan--Fossil Man of Mentone--Other remains near Mentone--Other bone caves of France--Belgian Caverns--Trou de Frontal--Trou Rosette-- Trou des Nutons--Cave of Chaleux--Cave at Furfooz--Cave of Thayngen--Cave near Cracow.

CHAPTER IX.

MAN OF THE REINDEER EPOCH.

Man under a more favorable aspect--Type of--Dwellings-- Clothing--Food--Cannibalism--The Arts--Traffic--Burial-- Dupont's Report.

CHAPTER X.

NEOLITHIC EPOCH.

How characterized--Caves of this period--Contents of--Cave of Saint Jean d'Alcas--Danish Shell-Mounds--Danish Peat Bogs--Lake-Dwellings of Switzerland--Enumeration of-- Robenhausen--Fauna and Flora of--Troyon and Keller on-- Other Lake-Dwellings--Chronology.

CHAPTER XI.

MAN OF THE NEOLITHIC.

CHAPTER XII.

BRONZE EPOCH.

CHAPTER XIII.

IRON EPOCH.

CHAPTER XIV.

TRACES OF MAN IN AMERICA.

CHAPTER XV.

WRITTEN HISTORY.

deposits of the Nile-- Dr. Schliemann's discoveries at Troy--History of Chaldea by Berosus--Astronomical calculations--Chinese history-- Mexican History.

CHAPTER XVI.

LANGUAGE.

A field for study--Three divisions of language--Rhematic period--Origin of-- Various theories--Change of--Views of Ancients--Number of--Comparative permancy of written language.

CHAPTER XVII.

UNITY OF THE HUMAN RACE.

Objections to the Unity of the Race--Anatomical-- Geographical--Disparity of--Non-existence of medium types-- Phenomena caused by two united types--Objections answered-- Both man and animals affected by climate, food, and condition--Examples--Argument from language--Ocean navigated by frail crafts--Examples--Captain Tyson and party--The two extremes exist in all nations, and even in families--People who have retrograded--Races will amalgamate and perpetuate their kind--Griquas--Papuas--Pitcairn Islanders-- Law of hybridity--Close affinity of the races--Slow change of.

CHAPTER XVIII.

THE BIBLE.

Controversy--Perversion of meaning--Men of science branded-- Design of the chapter--Creation--"Bara"--Day--Man's appearance--Two accounts--Case of Cain--Sons of God--Remarks of Dr. Livingstone--Doctrine of unity of the race-- Chronology--The Deluge--Septuagint--Monarchies--The Dispersion-- Opinion of Dr. Hedge--No supernatural aid in the formation of Language-- What God may do does not imply what he has done--Dean Stanley on the Biblical account of Creation.

A MANUAL OF THE ANTIQUITY OF MAN.

CHAPTER I.

INTRODUCTION.

No subject, of late years, has so much engrossed the attention of geologists as the antiquity of the human race. The interest was greatly increased by the publication of Sir Charles Lyell's "Antiquity of Man." This work called the attention of the public to the subject, and so great became the interest that many volumes and memoirs have been added to the list, discussing the question in various ways, and, for the most part, in such a manner as to add fresh interest and throw more light on the subject. The scientific men were slow to take advantage of the discoveries continually being made of the bones and works of man found in caves and associated with the remains' of extinct animals. It is probable, even at this late day, there would not have been so much discussion of this subject had not Sir Charles Lyell lent the weight of his great name to it. Educated men, everywhere, began to doubt the correctness of Archbishop Usher's chronology, and so complete has been the revolution of opinion that it is almost impossible to find an intelligent man who would limit the period of man's existence to 6,000 years.

To Aime Boue, a French geologist, must be attributed the honor of having been the first to proclaim the high antiquity of the human race; to Dr. Schmerling, the learned Belgian osteologist, on account of his laborious investigations, untiring zeal, and great work on the subject, the merited title of being the founder of the new science; to M. Boucher de Perthes, its great apostle; while to Sir Charles Lyell and Sir John Lubbock must be ascribed the honor of having made the new theory popular.

The new science soon became permanently established, and the geologists at once set about classifying the facts before them, in order to assign to them their respective places in the geological epochs. All are agreed in respect to the chronological orders, but all have not used the same nomenclature, in consequence of which more or less confusion has been the result. Sir J. Lubbock has divided pre-historic archaeology into four great epochs, as follows:

"I. That of the Drift; when man shared the possession of Europe with the mammoth, the cave-bear, the woolly-haired rhinoceros, and other extinct animals. This we may call the 'Palaeolithic' period.

"II. The later or polished Stone Age; a period characterized by beautiful stone weapons and instruments made of flint and other kinds of stone; in which, however, we find no trace of the knowledge of any metal, excepting gold, which seems to have been sometimes used for ornaments. This we may call the 'Neolithic' period.

"III. The Bronze Age, in which bronze was used for arms and cutting instruments of all kinds.

"IV. The Iron Age, in which that metal had superseded bronze for arms, axes, knives, etc."[1]

These divisions are recognized by Lyell and Tylor.

Edward Lartet has proposed the following classification:

I. THE STONE AGE.

1st. Epoch of extinct animals (or of the great bear and mammoth).

2d. Epoch of migrated existing animals (or the reindeer epoch).

3d. Epoch of domesticated existing animals (or the polished stone epoch).

II. THE METAL AGE.

1st. The Bronze Epoch.

2d. The Iron Epoch.

This mode of division is adopted by M. Figuier, in his "Primitive Man," by the Museum of Saint-Germain in that portion devoted to pre-historic antiquities, and adhered to in essential points by Troyon and d'Archiac.

Professor Renevier, of Lausanne, has proposed a somewhat different scheme, founded upon the epochs of Swiss glaciation. It is as follows:

"I. Pre-glacial Epoch, in which man lived cotemporaneously with the elephant (Elephas antiquus), rhinoceros (R. hemitaechus), and the cave-bear (Ursus spelaeus).

"II. Glacial Epoch, in which man lived cotemporaneously with the mammoth (Elephas primigenius), rhinoceros (R. tichorrhinus), cave-bear, etc.

"III. Post-glacial Epoch, in which man lived cotemporaneously with the mammoth and reindeer (Cervus tarandus).

"IV. Last Epoch, or epoch of the Pile-buildings, in which man lived cotemporaneously with the Irish elk (Megaceros hibernicus), aurochs (Bison Europaeus)," etc.[2]

Westropp divides the periods of man, in respect to his stages of civilization, as follows: Savagery, hunters, herdsmen, and agriculturists.

In the following pages a somewhat different classification has been adopted, and may be thus explained:

I. Pre-glacial Epoch; that period antedating the glaciers of the post-tertiary, in which man lived cotemporaneously with the animals of the tertiary, southern elephant (E. meridionalis), etc.

II. Glacial Epoch; that period of the post-tertiary when man was forced to contend with the great ice-fields and the floods immediately succeeding them, when the mammoth (E. primigenius), rhinoceros (R. tichorrhinus), cave-bear, etc., began to flourish.

III. Interglacial Epoch; that period between the glacial and the second advance of the ice, in which man lived cotemporaneously with the animals of the preceding epoch, and the cave bear became extinct.

IV. Reindeer Epoch; that period when the glaciers again advanced; in which man's chief food consisted of the flesh of the reindeer (C. tarandus), that animal having made its way in numerous herds as far south as the Pyrenees.

V. Neolithic Epoch; that period in which man polished his weapons of stone, and sought to domesticate certain animals, the dog, etc.

VI. Bronze Epoch; that period characterized by weapons and implements being made chiefly of bronze.

VII. Iron Epoch; that period in which bronze was generally superseded by iron.

This classification, on the whole, seems to be the best that could be devised, for the reason it attempts to place the evidences of the existence of man in their relative geological positions.

Other methods have misled the student. There was no universal Stone, Bronze, or Iron Age. The classification given by Lubbock applies to Europe, but is too general. I have adopted the word "Neolithic" for want of a better term, although the signification of the word is appropriate to the period it is intended to represent.

These various epochs are not sharply defined, the one from the other; but one merges into the other by gradual progression covering a period of thousands of years. The growth of the various plants and animals, and their retreat or final extinction, have also been very slow.

An outline of the history of the discoveries which led to a careful investigation of the question, and which resolved the question into a science, is not only one of interest but also of importance to the careful thinker seeking information on the subject.

Prior to the study of the ancient implements the "people had so little notion of the nature and signification of the stone axes and weapons of earlier and later times that they were regarded with superstitious fear and hope, and as productions of lightning and thunder. Hence for a long time they were called thunderbolts even by the learned.... As late as the year 1734 when Mahndel explained in the Academy of Paris that these stones were human implements, he was laughed at, because he had not proved that they could not have been formed in the clouds."[3]

As early as the year 1700, a human skull was dug out of the calcareous tuff of Constatt, in company with the bones of the mammoth. It is preserved in the Natural History Museum at Stuttgart.

In the year 1715, an Englishman named Kemp found in London, by the side of elephants' teeth, a stone hatchet, similar to those which have been subsequently found in great numbers in different parts of the world. This hatchet is still preserved in the British Museum.

In 1774, in the cavern of Gailenreuth, Bavaria, J. F. Esper discovered some human bones mingled with the remains of extinct animals.

In 1797, unpolished flint axes were dug out in great numbers from a brick-field near Hoxne, county of Suffolk, where they occurred at a depth of twelve feet, mingled with the bones of extinct species of animals. They were gathered up and thrown by basketsful upon the neighboring road. In the year 1801, before the Society of Antiquaries, John Frere read a paper upon them, in which he stated that they pointed to a very remote period. This communication, short as it was, contained the essence of all subsequent discoveries and speculations as to the antiquity of man. But the society regarded the subject as of no importance.

During the construction of a canal (1815-1823) in Hollerd, there was found, near Maestricht, in the loess, a human jaw in company with the bones of extinct animals. This bone is preserved in the museum at Leyden.

In 1823, Aime Boue disinterred portions of a human skeleton from ancient undisturbed loess near Lahr, a small village nearly opposite Strasbourg. These bones were placed in the care of Cuvier, but, having been neglected, are now lost.

In the same year, Dr. Buckland, an English geologist, published his "Reliquiae Diluvianae," a work principally devoted to a description of the Kirkdale Cave. The author combined all the known facts which favored the coexistence of man, with the extinct animals.

In 1828, M. Tournal and M. Christol explored numerous caverns in the south of France. In the cavern of Bize, Tournal found human bones and teeth, and fragments of rude pottery, together with the bones of both living and extinct species of animals, imbedded in the same mud and breccia, cemented by stalagmite. The human bones were in the same chemical condition as those of the extinct species.

M. Christol found in the cavern of Pondres, near Nimes, some human bones in the same mud with the bones of an extinct hyena and rhinoceros.

In 1833, Dr. Schmerling explored the two bone-caverns of Engis and Enghihoul (Belgium). In the former he found the Engis skull (now in the museum of the University of Liege), at a depth of nearly five feet, under an osseous breccia. The earth also contained the teeth of rhinoceros, horse, hyena, and bear, and exhibited no marks of disturbance. He also found the skull of a young person imbedded by the side of a mammoth's tooth. It was entire, but so fragile, that it fell to pieces before it was extracted. In the cave of Enghihoul he found numerous bones belonging to three human individuals, mingled with the bones of extinct animals. In these caves he noted rude flint instruments, but did not collect many of them. In the care of Chokier, he discovered a polished and jointed needle-shaped bone, with a hole pierced through it, at its base. The caves of Engis and Chokier have been annihilated, while only a part of Enghihoul remains.

Soon after these discoveries Dr. Schmerling published a work which described and represented a vast quantity of objects which had been discovered in the Belgian caverns. The scientific men were not yet prepared to receive the new discoveries, and it attracted but little attention at that time.

Too much praise cannot be bestowed upon Dr. Schmerling for his unremitting labors. Of these labors Sir Charles Lyell has said: "To have undertaken, in 1832, with a view of testing its truth (antiquity of fossil human bones) to follow the Belgian philosopher through every stage of his observations and proofs, would have been no easy task even for one well-skilled in geology and osteology. To be let down, as Schmerling was, day after day, by a rope tied to a tree, so as to slide to the foot of the first opening of the Engis cave, where the best-preserved human skulls were found; and, after thus gaining access to the first subterranean gallery, to creep on all fours through a contracted passage leading to larger chambers, there to superintend by torchlight, week after week and year after year, the workmen who were breaking through the stalagmitic crust as hard as marble, in order to remove piece by piece the underlying bone-breccia nearly as hard; to stand for hours with one's feet in the mud, and with water dripping from the roof on one's head, in order to mark the position and guard against the loss of each single bone of a skeleton; and at length, after finding leisure, strength, and courage for all these operations, to look forward, as the fruits of one's labor, to the publication of unwelcome intelligence, opposed to the prepossessions of the scientific as well as the unscientific public;--when these circumstances are taken into account, we need scarcely wonder.... that a quarter of a century should have elapsed before even the neighboring professors of the University of Liege came forth to vindicate the truthfulness of their indefatigable and clear-sighted countryman."[4]

In 1835, M. Joly, then professor at the Lyceum of Montpellier, found in the cave of Nabrigas (Lozere) the skull of a cave-bear, on which an arrow had left its mark. Close by, was a fragment of pottery marked by the finger of the moulder.

It was in the valley of the Somme (a river in the north of France) that M. Boucher de Perthes found those famous flint-axes of the rudest form. His explorations had been going on for a long time. He did all he could to bring these discoveries before the public. In the year 1836 he began to proclaim the high antiquity of man, in a series of communications addressed to the Societe d'Emulation of Abbeville. To the same society, in the year 1838, he exhibited the flint-axes he had found, but without result. In 1839, he took these hatchets to Paris, and showed them to some of the members of the Institute. At first they gave some encouragement toward these researches; but this favorable feeling did not last long. In 1841 he began to form his collection, which has since become so justly celebrated. He engaged trained workmen to dig in the diluvial beds, and in a short time he had collected twenty specimens of flint wrought by the hand of man, though in a very rude state. In 1846, he published his first work on the subject, entitled "De l'Industrie Primitive, ou les Arts et leur Origine." In the following year he published his "Antiquites Celtiques et Antediluviennes," in which he gave illustrations of these stone implements. This work attracted no attention until the year 1854, when a French savant, named Rigollot, made a personal examination and was successful in his search for these relicts in the neighborhood of Amiens. He was soon followed by Sir C. Lyell, Sir John Lubbock, Dr. Falconer, Sir Roderick I. Murchison, and other eminent scientists.

Boucher de Perthes, continuing his researches, was rewarded, in the year 1863, by finding the lower half of a human jaw bone, covered with an earthy crust, which he extracted with his own hands from a gravel-pit at Abbeville. A few inches from it a flint hatchet was discovered. They were at a depth of fifteen feet below the surface. This bone has been called the jaw of Moulin-Quignon, and is preserved in the Museum of Natural History at Paris.

The discovery of this bone produced a great sensation among English geologists. Christy, Falconer, Carpenter, and Busk went to France and examined the locality where the bone was found. They went away satisfied with both its authenticity and antiquity. Some geologists, however, doubted its authenticity; but at the present time all, or nearly all, recognize the truth of the conclusions of Boucher de Perthes.

Not far from the same locality, he was again successful, in 1869, in finding a number of human bones presenting the same character as the jaw of Moulin-Quignon.

In 1840, Rev. J. MacEnery, of Devonshire, England, found in a cave, called Kent's Hole, human bones and flint knives among the remains of the mammoth, cave-bear, hyena, and two-horned rhinoceros, all from under a crust of stalagmite. Mr. MacEnery began the explorations of this cave as early as 1825. He did not publish his notes on his discoveries but they remained in manuscript until 1859, when they were obtained by Mr. Vivian.

Mr. Godwin-Austen, in his communication to the Geological Society in the year 1840, states, in his description of Kent's Hole, he found works of art in all parts of the cave.

The fossil Man of Denise was discovered by a peasant, in an old volcanic tuff, near the town of Le Puy-en-Velay, Central France, an account of which was first published by Dr. Aymard, in 1844. Able naturalists, who have examined these bones, especially those familiar with the volcanic regions of Central

France, declared that they believed them to have been enveloped by natural causes in the tufaceous matrix in which they are now seen.

In the years 1845-1850, Casiano de Prado made discoveries on the banks of the Manzanares, near Madrid. They consisted of portions of the skeletons of the rhinoceros, and a nearly perfect skeleton of an elephant in the diluvial sand. Lying beneath this ossiferous sand, were several flint axes of human workmanship.

[Illustration: FIG. 1. SIR CHARLES LYELL.]

Near the town of Aurignac, France, a workman named Bonnemaison, in the year 1852, accidently discovered a cave containing the remains of seventeen human skeletons. These bones were taken by Dr. Amiel, the mayor of Aurignac, who was ignorant of their value, and consigned to the parish cemetery. The spot of their re-inhumation has been forgotten, and this treasure is now lost to science. In 1860, the cave was explored by Edward Lartet. After a long and patient examination, he came to the conclusion that the cave was a human burial place, cotemporary with the mammoth and other great animals of the quaternary epoch.

It was at the meeting of the British Association, in 1855, that Sir Charles Lyell declared his belief in the great antiquity of the human race. He had before opposed the idea, but was convinced of the truth by personal examination of human bones and flint hatchets, from the quarries of St. Acheul. He became enthusiastic in his investigations, and, in order to present the discussion clearly to the scientific public, he published his "Geological Evidences of the Antiquity of Man," in 1863. In the last edition of his "Principles of Geology," he bestows considerable space to the discussion of the subject. He was closely followed, in the same view, by other eminent geologists.

The remains of the ancient Lake Dwellings of Switzerland were discovered in the winter of 1853-1854. That winter was so dry and cold that the water of the lakes fell far below its ordinary level. On account of this, a large tract of ground of Lake Zurich was gained by the people throwing up embankments. In the process of the work, the piles on which stood the dwellings, fragments of pottery, bone and stone implements, and various other relics, were discovered.[5] Dr. Keller, of Zurich, examined the objects, and at once came to a right understanding as to their signification. He carefully examined the remains, and described these lake habitations in six memoirs presented to the Antiquarian Society of Zurich, in 1854, 1858, 1860, 1863, and 1866. In 1866 these memoirs were translated into English by J. E. Lee, together with articles from other antiquaries, under the title of "The Lake Dwellings of Switzerland, and other parts of Europe." This work contains ninety-seven plates, besides many wood-cuts.

Memoirs of the Dwellers of different lakes have, from time to time, been published, but they are included in the translated work of Dr. Keller.

The far-famed Neanderthal skull was discovered by Dr. Fuhlrott, in the year 1857, in a limestone cavern, near Duesseldorf, in a deep ravine known by the name of Neanderthal. This skull, with parts of the skeleton to which it belonged, was found under a layer of mud, about five feet in thickness. It is now in the cabinet of Dr. Fuhlrott, Elberfeld, Rhenish Prussia.

In 1858, a bone-cavern was found near Torquay, not far from Kent's Hole. This cave was examined by a scientific commission. At first it was undertaken by the Royal Society, but when its grants had failed, Miss Burdett-Coutts paid the expenses of completing the work. In this cave, under a layer of stalagmite, were found many flint knives, associated with the bones of extinct mammals.

M. A. Fontan found in the cave of Massat (Department of Ariege), in 1859, human teeth and utensils associated with the remains of the cave-bear, the fossil hyena, and the cave-lion (Felis speloea).

In 1861, M. A. Milne Edwards found certain relics of human industry mingled with the fossil bones of animals, in the cave of Lourdes, France.

In 1862, Dr. Garrigou published the result of the researches which he, in conjunction with Rames and Filhol, had made in the caverns of Ariege. These explorers found the jaw-bones of the cave-bear and cave-lion, which had been wrought by the hands of man.

In the upper strata of the tertiary beds (pliocene) at St. Prest (Department of Eure), in the year 1863, M. Desnoyers found the bones of extinct animals which were cut or notched by flint instruments. In the same strata Abbe

Bourgeois discovered implements of stone. He communicated his discoveries to the International Congress held at Paris in 1867.

In 1864, James Brown found flint implements midway between Gosport and Southampton, included in gravel from eight to twelve feet thick, capping a cliff which at its greatest height is thirty-five feet above high-water mark. These flint tools exactly resemble those found at Abbeville and Amiens. Some of them are preserved in the Blackmore Museum at Salisbury.

In 1865, there was found in the loess of the Rhine, near Colmar, Alsace, human bones in the same bed with bones of the mammoth, horse, stag, auroch, and other animals.

In 1866, Alfred Stevens first dug out a hatchet from the gravel at the top of the sea-cliff east of the Bournemouth opening, Southampton river. Soon after, Dr. Blackmore, to the west of the valley, obtained two other flint implements. The spot was examined by Lyell in 1867.

Dr. Edward Dupont, an eminent Belgian cave explorer, in the year 1866, found a fragment of a human jaw in the Trou de la Naulette, a bone cave situated on the bank of the river Lesse not far from Chaleux.

At the International Congress of 1867, M. A. Issel reported he had found several human bones in beds of Pliocene age, near Savonia, in Liguria.

The Reindeer Station on the Schusse, in Swabia, was discovered in 1867, during the operations undertaken for the improvement of a mill-pond. The Schusse is a little river which flows into the lake of Constance, and its source is upon the high plateau of Upper Swabia between the lake of Constance and the upper course of the Danube.

In 1868, Thomas Codrington discovered an oval flint implement in gravel at the top of the Foreland Cliff, Isle of Wight, five miles southeast of Ryde.

The fossil Man of Mentone was discovered, in 1873, by M. Riviere, in a cave near Nice, France. The skeleton was almost entire, and imbedded twenty feet below the surface of the deposit.

In 1873, M. Riviere discovered another human skeleton, by the side of which lay a few unpolished stone implements, in one of the caves in the same neighborhood.

In 1873 and 1874, M. Riviere was again so fortunate as to discover, in neighboring caves, the remains of three persons, two of them those of children. The skeletons were in the same condition, and decked with similar ornaments, as those he had previously discovered.

CHAPTER II.

GLACIAL EPOCH.

Happily for the Archaeo-geologist, there is given him a point from which to start in his researches into the antiquity of his race. Without it his calculations would be very indefinite and his efforts would be shorn of much of their interest. The Glacial Epoch, that has puzzled the mind of both the geologist and the astronomer, is a guide-post where he may not only look both ways, but also estimate the length of ages and number the years of man. Nothing, then, is of more importance, in this investigation, than an understanding of the condition of the earth prior to the glacial, and the knowledge of the date and length of this epoch.

For untold ages the earth, to all appearance, had been preparing itself for the reception of man. There was an abundance of game, the forests were beautiful, the domestic animals had made their appearance, the climate was warm, the soil rich, and the coal had been formed. Everything seemed to point to a bright and glorious future for man, who had already entered upon the scene. It is true there were fierce and savage beasts to contend with. These seemed but a motive power to stir man to action and develop the resources of his mind. Should he fail for a time to overcome the wild beasts a retreat was provided in the hollow recesses of the earth. But nature felt her work was still unfinished. The earth had passed through the ordeal of fire, and withstood the devastations of water, and now her long summer must come to an end. The arctic regions had been growing colder and colder, and the change was felt in the countries to the south. The northern animals were being clothed with a hairy or woolly garment for their protection. The aspect began to be forbidding. The future prospect of man was not only gloomy, but foreboded he should perish along with the many species of animals that were gradually succumbing to the cold. Great fields of ice were slowly accumulating at both the poles, and at last, by the power of their great weight, assisted by some geographical changes, began to move toward the equator, crushing and grinding the great rocks, and either driving before them, or else destroying, every living thing in their relentless march. Slowly but surely they moved on. The mountains groaned under the enormous weight of ice. Their heads were scarred, their sides bruised, torn and cut. The icy monsters listened not to the pleadings of earth, the lowing of cattle, or the cries of man. Centuries elapsed before the sun re-asserted his power. The rays of the sun, the internal heat of the earth, and other causes, produced a change. The northern ice was broken up by the time it reached latitude 39 deg. North America, leaving its indelible traces in the bowlders, gravel, beds of sand and clay which mark its course. In Europe this sheet of ice extended as far south as Spain and Corsica. The glaciers of the Antarctic regions extended as far as latitude 41 deg. south.

Fauna of Europe.--Among the Fauna may be mentioned the gigantic elephants, of nearly twice the bulk of the largest individuals that now exist, which roamed in herds over England, and extended across the Siberian plains and from Behring Strait to South Carolina. Two-horned rhinoceroses wallowed in the swamps of the ancient forests. Hippopotamuses inhabited the lakes and rivers. The great cave-bear, which sometimes attained the size of a horse, and the cave-tiger, twice as large as the living tiger, preyed upon the animals of less strength than themselves. Troops of hyenas, larger than those of South America, disputed with other beasts of prey. A species of wild-cat, lynx, and leopard found retreats in the same forests. Then there was a remarkable carnivorous animal called Machairodus, about the size of a tiger, and from the shape and size of the sword-like teeth, must have been a very destructive creature. The lemming and the musk ox found a home, and the wild horse pranced about unrestrained by the hand of man. The great Irish elks swiftly moved over the ground, and must have been very numerous, as their remains occur in abundance in peat-bogs and marl-pits. Nor should it be unmentioned that there was also a species of gigantic ox nearly as large as an elephant, that subsisted on the plains. All these animals followed the retreat of the glaciers and some of them were in close proximity to the ice.

Geological Period.--The glacial epoch occurred during the geological period known as the post-tertiary. The tertiary had gradually passed away and its time had been recorded on the pages of geological history. A new epoch began to dawn. This was the epoch of ice, the birth and almost the childhood of the post-tertiary.

Probable Date.--In discussing the probable date of the glacial epoch, Sir Charles Lyell says, "The attempt to assign a chronological value to any of our geological periods except the latest, must, in the present state of science, be hopeless. Nevertheless, independently of all astronomical considerations, it must, I think, be conceded that the period required for the coming on of the greatest cold, and for its duration when most intense, and the oscillations to which it was subject, as well as the retreat of the glaciers and the 'great thaw' or disappearance of snow from many mountain-chains where the snow was once perpetual, required not tens but hundreds of thousands of years. Less time would not suffice for the changes in physical geography and organic life of which we have evidence. To a geologist, therefore, it would not appear startling that the greatest cold should be supposed to have been two hundred thousand years ago, although this date must be considered as very conjectural, and one which may be as likely to err in deficiency of time as in excess."[6]

Sir John Lubbock, in his dissent from some calculations made by Mr. Geikie on the general effect produced by rivers in excavating valleys and lowering the general level of the country, says, "As regards the higher districts, however, his data are perhaps not far wrong, and if we apply them to the valley of the Somme, where the excavation is about two hundred feet in depth, they would indicate an antiquity for the palaeolithic epoch of from one hundred thousand to two hundred and forty thousand years."[7]

Dana, in his chapter on the length of geological time, says, in speaking of the time required to excavate the gorge of Niagara River, that "on both sides of the gorge near the whirlpool, and also at Goat Island, there are beds of recent lake shells ... the same kinds that live in still water near the entrance to the lake, and which are not found in the rapids. The lake, therefore, spread its still waters, when these beds were formed, over the gorge above the whirlpool. A tooth of a mastodon (M. giganteus) has been found in the same beds. This locates the time in the Champlain epoch.... Six miles of the gorge have been excavated since that mastodon was alive....

"There is a lateral valley leading from the whirlpool through the Queenstown precipice at a point a few miles west of Lewiston. This valley is filled with drift of the glacial epoch, and this blocking up of the channel may have compelled it to open a new passage.

"If, then, the falls have been receding six miles, and we can ascertain the probable rate of progress, we may approximate to the length of time it required. Hall and Lyell estimated the average rate at one foot a year,--which is certainly large. Mr. Desor concluded, after his study of the falls, that it was 'more nearly three feet a century than three feet a year.' Taking the rate at one foot a year, the six miles will have required over thirty-one thousand years; if at one inch a year--which is eight and one third feet a century--three hundred and eighty thousand years."[8]

The calculation made by Dana is for the Champlain epoch. As this epoch was subsequent to the glacial, the time must be either thrown still farther back, or else allow the calculations to begin with the end of the glacial.

Probable Duration.--Lyell has attempted to form an estimate of the duration of the glacial epoch by considering "the most simple series of changes in physical geography which can possibly account for the phenomena of the glacial period," and enumerates as follows:

"First, a continental period, toward the close of which the forest of Cromer flourished; when the land was at least five hundred feet above its present level, perhaps much higher, and its extent probably greater than that given in the map, Fig. 41." (In this map the whole of the British Isles are connected with one another, and with the continent--the German Ocean and the English Channel constituting dry land).

"Secondly, a period of submergence, by which the land north of the Thames and Bristol Channel, and that of Ireland, was gradually reduced to an archipelago; and finally to such a general prevalence of sea as is seen in map, Fig. 39." (This map is intended to represent the British Isles as they appeared above water when Scotland was submerged to two thousand feet and other parts of the isles to one thousand three hundred feet.) "This was the period of submergence and of floating ice, when the Scandinavian flora, which occupied the lower grounds during the first continental period, may have obtained exclusive possession of the only lands not covered with perpetual snow.

"Thirdly, a second continental period, when the bed of the glacial sea, with its marine shells and erratic blocks, was laid dry, and when the quantity of land equalled that of the first period.... During this period there were glaciers in the higher mountains of Scotland and Wales....

"The submergence of Wales to the extent of one thousand four hundred feet, as proved by glacial shells, would require fifty-six thousand years, at the rate of two and a half feet per century; but taking Professor Ramsay's estimate of eight hundred feet more, that depression being required for the deposition of some of the stratified drift, we must demand an additional period of thirty-two thousand years, amounting in all to eighty-eight thousand; and the same time would be required for the reelevation of the tract to its present height. But if the land rose in the second continental period no more than six hundred above the present level ... this ... would have taken another twenty-six thousand years; the whole of the grand oscillation, comprising the submergence and reemergence, having taken, in round numbers, two hundred and twenty-four thousand years for its completion; and this, even if there were no pause or stationary period, when the downward movement ceased, and before it was converted into an upward one."[9]

Lyell admits that the average rate of two and a half feet per century is a purely arbitrary and conjectural one, and there are cases where the change is even six feet a century, yet the average rate of motion, he thinks, will not exceed that above proposed. With this opinion, Lubbock believes most geologists will agree.[10]

By the estimates already given a basis is formed upon which a calculation can be made as to the time when this epoch began. At the time of the most intense cold the eccentricity of the earth's orbit was .0575; the difference in millions of miles between the greatest and least distances of the earth from the sun 10-1/2; the number of days by which winter, occurring in aphelion was longer than the summer in perihelion 27.8; the mean temperature of the hottest summer month in the latitude of London when the summer occurs in perihelion, 113 deg.; the mean temperature of the coldest winter month in the latitude of London when the winter occurs in aphelion, 0 deg. 7'. Sixty thousand years later the eccentricity of the earth's orbit was but .0332; the difference of distance in millions of miles was 6; number of winter days in excess, 16.1; mean of hottest month in latitude of London, 95 deg., and mean of coldest month 12 deg.. It is evident then at this time (one hundred and fifty thousand years ago) a "great thaw" had taken place and the glaciers driven back, although fifty thousand years later less intense cold set in again. If thirty thousand years be allowed for the "great thaw" from the extreme point of cold, and that extreme point to have been two hundred and ten thousand years ago, then one hundred and eighty thousand years ago the glaciers had become so broken up as to allow vegetation to spring up in many localities, and the wild beasts to partially reassert their dominion. If to this be added the time required for the duration of the glacial epoch (two hundred and twenty-four thousand years) then the time when the ice began to accumulate was four hundred and four thousand years ago. But if the tables of Mr. Croll be correct, their beginning could not have been earlier than three hundred and fifty thousand years ago, as the eccentricity of the earth's orbit varied but little from the present, and five hundred and fifty thousand years ago it was almost identical with that of the present.[11]

During the last stages of this ocean of ice it must have melted very rapidly,[12] for great rivers were formed, and the water pouring down its icy bed sought other streams, and on the bosom of the earth swept away loose sediment, depositing it along the course of rivers and in caves of the earth, covering the remains of man along with those of animals that perished during the long winter of ice.

[Illustration: FIG. 2. STREAM ISSUING FROM A GLACIER.]

Evidences of the Existence of Man.--The traces of man in the deposits made during the glacial epoch are numerous. Out of the many, the most noted will be given, with a view to their chronological order.

In all probability the very oldest implements of the post-tertiary, and consequently the beginning of the glacial epoch, if not of the pliocene, are those found in the south of Hampshire, between Gosport and Southampton. They came from a tabular mass of drift which caps the tertiary strata. "The great bed of gravel resting on eocene tertiary strata, in which these implements have been found, consists in most places of half-rolled or semi-angular chalk flints, mixed with rounded pebbles washed out of the tertiary strata.... Many of them exhibit the same colors and ochreous stain as do the flints in the gravel in which they lay."

West of the Southampton estuary, "on both sides of the opening at Bournemouth, flint tools of the ancient type have been met with in the gravel capping the cliffs. The gravel from which the flint tool was taken at Bournemouth is about one hundred feet above the level of the sea.... The gravel consists in great part of pebbles derived from tertiary strata."

The oval flint implement discovered in gravel at the top of the Foreland cliff "is of the true palaeolithic type, and the gravel in which it is imbedded at the height of about eighty feet above the level of the sea, may have once extended to the cliffs near Gosport; in which case we should have to infer that the channel called the Solent had not yet been scooped out when this region was inhabited by palaeolithic man."[13]

It may be safely inferred that the implements in the above three enumerations were imbedded at about the same time.

The flint implements from the valley of the Somme, which have been of so much interest, and convinced so many sceptical geologists, belong to the early part of this epoch. This valley may be represented by Fig. 3.

[Illustration: FIG. 3. SECTION ACROSS THE SOMME IN PICARDY.

1. Peat, twenty to thirty feet thick, resting on gravel, a.

2. Lower level gravel, with elephants' bones and flint tools covered with fluviatile loam, twenty to forty feet thick.

3. Upper level gravel, with similar fossils, and overlying loam. In all thirty feet thick.

4. Upland loam without shells, five or six feet thick.

5. Eocene tertiary strata, resting on the chalk in patches.]

In explanation of the above it may be well to remark that No. 2 indicates the lower level gravels, and No. 3 the higher ones, which are from eighty to one hundred feet above the river. Of a later date than these is the peat, No. 1, which is from ten to thirty feet in thickness. Underneath the peat is a bed of gravel, a, from three to fourteen feet thick, resting on undisturbed chalk. But between the gravel and the peat is a thin layer of impervious clay. This section of the valley of the Somme is a pretty fair representation of the arrangements of the different beds at Abbeville, Amiens, and and St. Acheul.

In these beds are the records of two drift periods, marked by 2 and 3. The two are separated by a layer of fresh-water deposits, which contains river shells and is sometimes as much as sixteen feet thick. The lower, or gray diluvium, (No. 2), marks the glacial epoch, as distinct from the glaciers of the reindeer epoch. In the lower gravel, lying immediately upon the tertiary formation, were found the flint hatchets, together with the bones of the mammoth and fossil rhinoceros.

In order to understand the deposits still more clearly, the following figure is given.

[Illustration: FIG. 4. SECTION OF A GRAVEL-PIT AT ST. ACHEUL.

1. Vegetable and made soil from two to three feet thick.

2. Brown loam from four to five feet thick, containing a few angular flints.

3. Bed of sandy marl from five to six feet thick, with land and fresh-water shells, covered with a thin layer of angular gravel from one to two feet thick.

4. A bed of partially rounded gravel containing well-rolled tertiary pebbles. In this bed the flint implements are chiefly found--ten to fourteen feet thick.

5. Formation of chalk. a. Part of elephant's molar, eleven feet from surface. b. Entire molar of mammoth (E primigenius), seventeen feet from surface. c. Position of flint hatchet, eighteen feet from surface. d. Gravel projecting five feet.]

At St. Acheul, in bed No. 4, were found large numbers of flint implements. Some of them have the shape of a spear-head, and are over seven inches in length. The oval-shaped hatchets are so rude in some instances as to require a practised eye to decide their human origin. In the same bed are found small round bodies having a tubular cavity in the centre. Dr. Rigollot has suggested that these perforated stones or gravel were used as ornaments, possibly strung together as beads.

In this bed, No. 4, seventeen feet from the surface, was found a mammoth's tooth. About one foot below the tooth, in densely compressed gravel, was found a stone hatchet of an oval form.

[Illustration: FIG. 5. FLINT IMPLEMENT FROM ST. ACHEUL.

Half the size of the original, which is seven and a half inches long.

a. Side view. b. Same seen edgewise.

"These spear-headed implements have been found in greater number, proportionally to the oval ones, in the upper level gravel at St. Acheul, than in any of the lower gravels in the valley of the Somme. In these last, the oval form predominates, especially at Abbeville."--Antiquity of Man, p. 114.]

That this bed was formed by action of glaciers is shown, not only from the well-rounded tertiary pebbles, but also from the great blocks of hard sandstone, some of which are over four feet in diameter. These large fragments not only abound at St. Acheul in both the higher and lower level gravels at Amiens, and at the higher level at Abbeville, but they are also traced far up the valley wherever the old diluvium occurs. All of these sandstones have been derived from the tertiary strata which once covered the chalk.

[Illustration: FIG. 6. FLINT IMPLEMENT FROM ABBEVILLE.

a. Oval-shaped flint hatchet from Mautort near Abbeville, half size of original, which is five and a half inches long, from a bed of gravel underlying the fluvio-marine stratum.

b. Same seen edgewise.

c. Shows a recent fracture of the edge of the same at the point a, or near the top. This portion of the tool, c, is drawn of the natural size, the black central part being the unaltered flint, the white outer coating, the layer which has been formed by discoloration or bleaching since the tool was first made.

The entire surface of Figure 6 must have been black when first shaped, and the bleaching to such a depth must have been the work of time, whether produced by exposure to the sun and air before it was imbedded, or afterward when it lay deep in the soil.--Antiquity of Man.]

As the flint implements of Abbeville and Amiens are the same as those of St. Acheul, and from the same beds, what has already been said will apply to them. These implements have been found in these localities in great numbers, as several thousand of them already taken from the beds will amply testify.

From the gravel-pit in which were found the flint axes, at Abbeville, and close to the ancient chalk, was taken the celebrated human bone known as the jaw of Moulin-Quignon. It was cotemporary with the axes, and undoubtedly some of the flint implements there found were fashioned by the man of whom that jaw formed so necessary a part.

This jaw-bone belonged to an old man, and is described as displaying "a tendency toward the animal structure in the shortness and breadth of the ascending ramus (the perpendicular portion of the lower jaw), the equal height of the two apophyses (a process or regular prominence forming a continuous part of the body of the bone), the indication of prognathism (projecting jaw) furnished by the very obtuse angle at which the ramus joins the body of the bone.[14]

Near the same locality other human bones were discovered Which presented the same characteristics.

Boucher de Perthes having pointed out that flint implements could be found in the valley of the Seine, in beds similar to those of Abbeville, the antiquaries were soon rewarded and Boucher de Perthes' prediction was fulfilled. M.

Gosse, of Geneva, found the Abbeville type of implements in the lowest diluvial deposits associated with the remains of animals of that period.

The discovery made by Casiano de Prado, near Madrid, is very similar to those of Abbeville. "First, vegetable soil; then about twenty-five feet of sand and pebbles, under which was a layer of sandy loam, in which, during the year 1850, a complete skeleton of the mammoth was discovered. Underneath this stratum was about ten feet of coarse gravel, in which some flint axes, very closely resembling those of Amiens, have been discovered."[15]

The remains of man are also preserved in caverns associated with the fossil bones of the mammoth, the woolly-haired rhinoceros, cave-bear, and other extinct quadrupeds. Among these should be noticed Kent's Hole, which has furnished a mine of wealth. Of his discoveries Godwin-Austen says: "Human remains and works of art, such as arrow-heads and knives of flint, occur in all parts of the cave, and throughout the entire thickness of the clay; and no distinction founded on condition, distribution, or relative position can be observed, whereby the human can be separated from the other reliquiae," which included bones of the mammoth (E. primigenius), rhinoceros (R. tichorrhinus), cave-bear (Ursus spelaeus), cave-hyena (H. spelaeus), and other mammalia. These researches were conducted in parts of the cave which had never been disturbed, and the works of man, in every instance, were procured from undisturbed loam or clay, beneath a thick covering of stalagmite; and all these must have been introduced before the stalagmite flooring had been formed.[16] These specimens of man's handicraft were found far below the stalagmite floor.[17] Closely allied to Kent's Hole is Brixham Cave. The following gives the general succession of deposits forming the contents of the cavern:

1. A layer of stalagmite varying from one to fifteen inches in thickness.

2. Next below, ochreous cave-earth, from one foot to fifteen feet in thickness.

3. Rounded gravel, in some places more than twenty feet in depth.

In the second layer there were found the remains of the mammoth, rhinoceros, cave-bear, cave-hyena, cave-lion, reindeer, and seven other species. Indiscriminately mixed with these bones were found many flint knives, but chiefly from the lowest part of the ochreous cave-earth, varying in depth from ten inches to thirteen feet. The antiquity of these cannot be doubted, from the simple fact, even if there was no other, that in close proximity to a very perfect flint tool was discovered the entire left hind leg of a cave-bear, and every bone in its natural position. From the bone earth there were taken fifteen knives, recognized, by the experienced antiquaries, as having been artificially formed. In the lowest gravel, underlying all, there were found imperfect specimens of flint knives. The fine layer of mud was deposited by the slow but regular action of water. Since these layers were formed the stream has cut its channel seventy-eight feet below its former level.[18]

On both banks of the Meuse, at Maestricht (Hollerd) are terraces of gravel covered with loess. Below the city, on the left bank, one of these terraces projects into the alluvial plain of the Meuse. During the construction of the canal the terrace was opened to a depth of sixty feet. The upper twenty feet consisted of loess and the lower forty feet of stratified gravel. Great numbers of molars, tusks, and bones of elephants, together with those of other mammalia, and a human lower jaw with teeth, were found in or near this gravel. The human jaw was at a depth of nineteen feet from the surface, in a stratum of sandy loam, beneath a stratum of pebbly and sandy beds, and immediately above the gravel. The stratum from which the jaw was taken was intact and had never been disturbed. But the jaw was somewhat isolated, and the nearest fossil object was the tusk of an elephant six yards distant, though on a horizontal plane. This fossil is probably older than that discovered at Lahr. It was probably covered just before the gush of the water when it first began to flow from the gorges and had washed the ground at some distance from the ice.[19]

The human skeleton from the undisturbed loess of the Rhine, near Lahr, was found in nearly a horizontal position, but in such a manner as to forbid the idea of sepulchre. These bones were exhumed from a perpendicular cliff of solid loess, about five feet high. The town of Lahr is situated four miles from, and about one hundred feet above, the Rhine, and not far from the tributary valley drained by the Schutter, flowing from the Black Forest.

In the alluvial plain into which the Schutter flows the the loess is two hundred feet thick. The loess rises eighty feet above the Schutter. At Lahr it has been denuded so as to form a succession of terraces on the right bank. It was in the lowest of these from which the skeleton was taken. Immediately below this bed there were found pebbles, and still lower down was a bed of gravel containing rounded stones of sandstone and gneiss from the Black Forest.

There are several interesting facts connected with this discovery. M. Boue considers that the loess of the Lahr is continuous with that of the Rhine, and before the loess had been denuded there was not less than eighty feet of loamy deposit above the human skeleton. The glaciers had deposited their great gravel beds, and had began to melt. The melting of them had formed a mixture of loam and gravel. Then when the torrents poured forth from the glaciers the loam was formed without the pebbles. The unfortunate man, whose remains were found, was buried far beneath the surface, during the very first part of the course of the violent streams pouring forth from the field of ice. The glaciers were then on the retreat, and the incautious man probably fell a victim while on the chase.[20]

The cave of La Naulette, Belgium, afforded a jaw-bone similar to the Moulin-Quignon. The bone came from a river deposit of loam covered with a layer of stalagmite, and at a depth of thirteen feet from the surface. Associated with it were the remains of the mammoth, woolly-haired rhinoceros, and flint implements. These implements present the same type as those of St. Acheul. With this jaw were also found a human ulna, two human teeth, and a fragment of a worked reindeer born. This jaw-bone is very thick, round in form, and the projection of the chin is almost entirely absent. The chin is said to hold an intermediate position between that of the animals and those of the present race of men. The cavities for the reception of the canine teeth are very wide, and one of the most remarkable things is that the three molars are reversed, that is the first true molar is the smallest, and the last the largest. The inner surface of the jaw at the point of the suture or symphysis, forms a line obliquely directed upwards. Taking the jaw all in all, it is the most ape-like human jaw ever discovered.[21]

The flint implements from Hoxne were found under three different layers or beds. The first, vegetable, a foot and a half in depth. The second was clay, seven and a half feet thick. The third, a bed of sand, with shells one foot in thickness. The fourth layer, containing the implements was a bed of gravel two feet in depth. The number of these flints was so great that they were carried out by the baskets-full, and thrown into the ruts of the adjoining road. On account of the great number, this spot might have been the place where they were manufactured. Their date is not coeval with the bowlder clay, but undoubtedly belong, to the last of this epoch.

The human bones found in the loess of the Rhine, near Colmar, were two fossilized fragments of the skull. They were found in undisturbed soil along with the fossil bones of the extinct species of mammoth, horse, gigantic deer, aurochs, and other mammalia. The fragment of the skull "showed a depressed forehead, strongly projecting superciliary arches, and a type, on the whole, approaching the so-called dolichocephalic, or long-headed form."[22] These remains date so near the end of the glacial as to almost enter the inter-glacial.

CHAPTER III.

GLACIAL EPOCH--CONTINUED.

Belgian Caverns.--The relics discovered by Dr. Schmerling, in the caves of Belgium, must be referred to the time of the retreat of the glaciers. The glaciers were still in existence, but their receding had freed immense tracts of land, and the space they now covered was small in proportion to their former extent. Whether it be considered or not, that vegetation greatly nourished and the great wild beasts were rapidly increasing, one thing must be noticed, and that is, floods must have succeeded or followed closely upon the retreat of the ice. Many remains, referred to the glacial epoch, may in reality, have occupied the time of the floods occurring just previous to the commencement of the inter-glacial.

The Belgian Caverns, near Liege, either belong exactly to the ice, or else to a period not far removed. Lyell considers the older monuments of the palaeolithic period to be the rude implements found in ancient river gravel and in the mud and stalagmite caves.[23] Caves of this description are those reported on by Dr. Schmerling.

The caverns of the province of Liege were not the dens of wild beasts, but their contents had been swept in by the action of water. The bones of man "were of the same color, and in the same condition as to the amount of animal matter contained in them, as those of the accompanying animals, some of which, like the cave-bear, hyena, elephant, and rhinoceros, were extinct; others, like the wild-cat, beaver, wild boar, roe-deer, wolf, and hedgehog, still extant. The fossils were lighter than fresh bones, except such as had their pores filled with carbonate of lime, in which case they were often much heavier. The human remains of most frequent occurrence were teeth detached from the jaw, and the carpal, metacarpal, tarsal, metatarsal, and phalangial bones separated from the rest of the skeleton. The corresponding bones of the cave-bear, the most abundant of the accompanying mammalia, were also found in the Liege caverns more commonly than any others, and in the same scattered condition."[24] In some of these caves, rude flint implements, of a triangular form, were found dispersed through the cave mud. Dr. Schmerling did not pay much attention to these, as he was engrossed in his osteological inquiries. The human bones were met with at all depths, in the cave mud and gravel, both above and below those of the extinct mammalia.

The floors of these caverns were incrusted with stalagmite.[25] In the cavern at Chokier there occur "three distinct beds of stalagmite, and between each of them a mass of breccia, and mud mixed with quartz pebbles, and in the three deposits the bones of extinct quadrupeds."[26]

FOSSIL SKULL OF THE ENGIS CAVE NEAR LIEGE.

The fossil skull from the cavern of Engis was deposited at a depth of about five feet, under an osseous breccia containing a tusk of the rhinoceros, the teeth of the horse, and the remains of small animals. The breccia was about three and one-fourth feet wide, and rose to the height of about five feet above the floor of the cavern. In the earth which contained the skull there was found, surrounding it on all sides, the teeth of the rhinoceros, horse, hyena, and bear, and with no marks of the earth having been disturbed.

There was also found the cranium of a young person, in the floor of the cavern, besides an elephant's tooth. When first observed, the skull was entire, but fell to pieces when removed from its position. Besides these there were found a fragment of a superior maxillary bone, with the molar teeth worn down to the roots, indicating that of an old man; two vertebrae, a first and last dorsal; a clavicle of the left side, belonging to a young individual of great stature; two fragments of the radius, indicating a man of ordinary height; a fragment of an ulna: some metacarpal bones; six metatarsal, three phalanges of the hand and one of the foot.

Dr. Schmerling found in this cave a pointed bone implement incrusted with stalagmite and joined to a stone.

Of the Engis skull Professor Huxley has remarked, "As Professor Schmerling observes, the base of the skull is destroyed, and the facial bones are entirely absent; but the roof of the cranium, consisting of the frontal, parietal, and the greater part of the occipital bones, as far as the middle of the occipital foramen, is entire, or nearly so. The left temporal bone is wanting. Of the right temporal, the parts in the immediate neighborhood of the auditory foramen, the mastoid process, and a considerable portion of the squamous element of the temporal, are well preserved."

A piece of the occipital bone, which Schmerling seems to have missed, has since been fitted on to the rest of the cranium by Dr. Spring, the accomplished anatomist of Liege.

"The skull is that of an adult, if not middle-aged man. The extreme length of the skull is 7.7 inches. Its extreme breadth, which corresponds very nearly with the interval between the parietal protuberances, is not more than 5.4 inches. The proportion of the length to the breadth is therefore very nearly as 100 to 70. If a line be drawn from the point at which the brow curves in towards the root of the nose, and which is called the 'glabella' (a, Fig. 8), to the occipital protuberance (d), and the distance to the highest point of the arch of the skull be measured perpendicularly from this line, it will be found to be 4.75 inches. Viewed from above, the forehead presents an evenly rounded curve, and passes into the contour of the sides and back of the skull, which describes a tolerably regular elliptical curve.

[Illustration: FIG. 7. PROFESSOR T. H. HUXLEY.]

[Illustration: FIG. 8. SIDE VIEW OF THE HUMAN SKULL FOUND IN THE CAVE

a. Superciliary ridge and glabella. b. Coronal suture. d. The occipital protuberance.]

"The front view shows that the roof of the skull was very regularly and elegantly arched in the transverse direction, and that the transverse diameter was a little less below the parietal protuberances, than above them. The forehead cannot be called narrow in relation to the rest of the skull, nor can it be called a retreating forehead; on the contrary, the antero-posterior contour of the skull is well arched, so that the distance along that contour, from the nasal depression to the occipital protuberance, measures about 13.75 inches. The transverse arc of the skull, measured from one auditory foramen to the other, across the middle of the sagittal suture, is about 13 inches. The sagittal suture itself is 5.5 inches long. The superciliary prominences or brow-ridges (a) are well, but not excessively, developed, and are separated by a median depression. Their principal elevation is disposed so obliquely that I judge them to be due to large frontal sinuses. If a line joining the glabella and the occipital protuberance (a, d, Fig. 8) be made horizontal, no part of the occipital region projects more than one-tenth of an inch behind the posterior extremity of that line, and the upper edge of the auditory foramen is almost in contact with a line drawn parallel with this upon the outer surface of the skull."[27]

Some of the views expressed by Professor Huxley are at variance with those of other eminent scientists. Lubbock reports him as saying, "There is no mark of degradation about any part of its structure. It is, in fact, a fair average human skull, which might have belonged to a philosopher, or might have contained the thoughtless brains of a savage."[28] Mr. Busk agrees and partially disagrees with Professor Huxley, for he remarked to Lyell, "Although the forehead was somewhat narrow, it might nevertheless be matched by the skulls of individuals of European race."[29]

Dr. Schmerling, Buchner, and Vogt are arrayed against Huxley. The first says, "I hold it to be demonstrated that this cranium has belonged to a person of limited intellectual faculties, and we conclude thence that it belonged to a man of a low degree of civilization."[30] "From the narrowness of the frontal portion it belonged to an individual of small intellectual development."[31]

Buchner says, "In its length and narrowness, the slight elevation of its forehead, the form of the widely separated orbits and the well developed supra-orbital arches, it resembles, especially when viewed from above, the celebrated Neanderthal skull, but in general is far superior to this in its structure."[32] Carl Vogt "regards it, with reference to the proportion of length to breadth, as one of the most ill-favored, animal-like and simian of skulls."[33]

The cause of this wide difference of opinion may arise from the failure to observe the fact that the older the formation in which a skull is found, the lower is the type. The ordinary observer, judging by the cast of the skull, would see nothing ape-like about it, and certainly would fail to see any indications of a philosopher.

NEANDERTHAL SKULL.

The Neanderthal skull was taken from a small cave or grotto in-the valley of the Duessel, near Duesseldorf, situated about seventy miles north-east of the region of the Liege caverns. The grotto is in a deep ravine sixty feet above the river, one hundred feet below the surface of the country, and at a distance of about ten feet from the Duessel River. It is fifteen feet deep from the entrance (f), which is seven or eight feet wide. Before the cavern had been injured, it opened upon a narrow plateau lying in front. The floor of the cave was covered four or five feet in thickness with a deposit of mud or loam, and containing some rounded fragments of chert. Two laborers, in removing this deposit, first noticed the skull, placed near the entrance, and further in met with the other bones. As the bones were not regarded as of any importance, at the time of their discovery, only the larger ones have been preserved.

[Illustration: FIG. 9. SECTION OF THE NEANDERTHAL CAVE.

a. Cavern sixty feet above the Duessel, and one hundred feet below the surface of the country at c.

b. Loam covering the floor of the cave near the bottom of which the human skeleton was found.

c, a. Rent connecting the cave with the upper surface of the country.

d. Superficial sandy loam.

e. Devonian limestone.

f. Terrace, or ledge of rock.]

Some discussion has arisen in respect to the geological time of these bones. There was no stalagmite overlying the mud or loam in which the skeleton was found, and no other bones met with save the tusk of a bear. There is no certain data given whereby its position may be known. Professor Huxley declares that the bones "indicate a very high antiquity."[34] Buchner is very positive in his statement, and declares that "the loam-deposit which partly fills the caves of the Neanderthal and the clefts and fissures of its limestone mountains, and in which both the Neanderthal bones and the fossil bones and teeth of animals were imbedded, is exactly the same that, in the caverns of the Neanderthal, covers the whole limestone mountain with a deposit from ten to twelve feet in thickness, and the diluvial origin of which is unmistakable."[35] Dr. Fuhlrott says, "The position and general arrangement of the locality in which they were found, place it, in my judgment, beyond doubt that the bones belong to the diluvium, and therefore to primitive times, i. e. they come down to us from a period of the past when our native country was still inhabited by various kinds of animals, especially mammoths and cave-bears, which have long since disappeared out of the series of living creatures."[36]

The diluvial or glacial origin of the Neanderthal skull is still further confirmed by the discoveries made, in the summer of 1865, in the Teufelskammer. This cavern is situated one hundred and thirty paces from the one in which the human bones were found, and on the same side of the river.. In the loam-deposit of this cave were found numerous fossil bones and teeth of the rhinoceros, cave-bear, cave-hyena, and other extinct animals. "A great part of these bones, especially those of the cave-bears, agree in color, weight, density, and the preservation of their microscopic structure, with the human bones found in the Feldhofner Cave (in which the Neanderthal man was found), and both are covered with the same dendrites, or tree-like markings."[37]

Before entering into a description and discussion of this remarkable skull, an enumeration of the other bones will be given. All the bones are characterized by their unusual thickness, and the great development of all the elevations and depressions for the attachment of muscles. The two thigh bones were in a perfect state, also the right humerus and radius; the upper third of the right ulna; the left ulna complete, though pathologically deformed, the coronoid process being so much enlarged by bony growth that flexure of the elbow beyond a right angle was impossible; the left humerus is much slenderer than the right, and the upper third is wanting. Its anterior fossa for the reception of the coronoid process is filled up with a bony growth, and, at the same time, the olecranon process is curved strongly downwards. The indications are that an injury sustained during life was the cause of this defect. There was an ilium, almost perfect; a fragment of the right scapula; the anterior extremity of a rib of the right side, and two hinder portions and one middle portion of ribs resembling more the ribs of a carnivorous animal than those of man. This abnormal condition has arisen from the powerful development of the thoracic muscles.

[Illustration: FIG. 10. SIDE VIEW OF THE HUMAN SKULL FROM FELDHOFNER CAVE, IN THE NEANDERTHAL, NEAR DUeSSELDORF.

a. The superciliary ridge and glabella. c. The apex of the lambdoidal suture. b. The coronal suture. d. The occipital protuberance.]

The cranium is thus described by Professor Huxley. "It has an extreme length of 8 inches, while its breadth is only 5-3/4 inches, or in other words, its length is to its breadth as 100 is to 72. It is exceedingly depressed, measuring only about 3.4 inches from the glabello-occipital line to the vertex. The longitudinal arc, measured in the same way as in the Engis skull, is 12 inches; the transverse arc cannot be exactly ascertained, in consequence of the absence of the temporal bones, but was probably about the same, and certainly exceeded 10-1/4 inches. The horizontal circumference is 23 inches. But this great circumference arises largely from the vast development of the superciliary ridges, though the perimeter of the brain case itself is not small. The large superciliary ridges give the forehead a far more retreating appearance than its internal contour would bear out. To an anatomical eye the posterior part of the skull is even more striking than the anterior. The occipital protuberance occupies the extreme posterior end of the skull, when the glabello-occipital line is made horizontal, and so far from any part of the occipital region extending beyond it, this region of the skull slopes obliquely upward and forward, so that the lambdoidal suture is situated well upon the upper surface of the cranium. At the same time, notwithstanding the great length of the skull, the sagittal suture is remarkably short (4-1/2 inches) and the squamosal suture is very straight."[38] ... "The cranium, in its present condition, contains about sixty-three English cubic inches of water. As the entire skull could hardly have held less than twelve cubic inches more, its minimum capacity may be estimated at seventy-five cubic inches.... It has certainly not undergone compression, and, in reply to the suggestion that the skull is that of an idiot, it may be urged that the onus probandi lies with those who adopt the hypothesis. Idiocy is compatible with very various forms and capacities of the cranium, but I know of none which present the least resemblance to the Neanderthal skull."[39]

Professor Huxley describes this skull to be the most ape-like of all the human skulls he has ever seen, and in its examination ape-like characters are met with in all its parts.[40] Buchner says that the face of the Neanderthal man must have presented a frightfully bestial and savage, or ape-like expression (see frontispiece).[41] Professor Schaaffhausen and Mr. Busk have stated that "this skull is the most brutal of all known human skulls, resembling those of the apes not only in the prodigious development of the superciliary prominences and the forward extension of the orbits, but still more in the depressed form of the brain-case, in the straightness of the squamosal suture, and in the complete retreat of the occiput forward and upward, from the superior occipital ridges."[42]

Professor Schaaffhausen and Dr. Buchner regarded this skull as a race-type, and Professor Huxley has said "that it truly forms only the extreme member of a series leading by slow degrees to the highest and best developed forms of human skulls."[43]

That this skull is a race-type is evident from the fact that it is not an isolated case. The fragment of the skull from the loess of the Rhine (Alsace), by its depressed forehead and strongly projecting superciliary arches, greatly resembles the Neanderthal skull. The skull from the calcareous tuff of Constatt, in its low, narrow forehead and strong superciliary arches, resembles the Neanderthal.[44] The cranium found in bone breccia, in

Cochrane's Cave (Gibraltar), "resembles, in all essential particulars, including its great thickness, the far-famed Neanderthal skull. Its discovery adds immensely to the scientific value of the Neanderthal specimen, if only as showing that the latter does not represent, as many have hitherto supposed, a mere individual peculiarity, but that it may have been characteristic of a race extending from the Rhine to the Pillars of Hercules."[45] In speaking of the Neanderthal skull, Professor Schaaffhausen says, "It is worthy of notice that a similar, although smaller projection of the superciliary arches has generally been found in the skulls of savage races.... The remarkably small skull from the graves on the island of Moen, examined by Professor Eschricht; the two human skulls, described by Dr. Kutorga, from the government of Minsk (Russia), one of which, especially, shows a great resemblance to the Neanderthal skull; the human skeleton found near Plau, in Mecklenburg, in a very ancient grave, in a squatting position, ... the skull of which indicates a very distant period, when man stood on a very low grade of development;" and other similar discoveries near Mecklenburg, their skulls likewise presenting short, retreating foreheads and projecting eyebrows.[46]

Professor Huxley considers that the Borreby skulls, belonging to the stone age of Denmark, "show a great resemblance to the Neanderthal skull, a resemblance which is manifested in the depression of the cranium, the receding forehead, the contracted occiput and the prominent superciliary ridges."[47]

Human Skull of Arno.--The human skull, found by Professor Cocchi in the valley of the Arno, near Florence, in diluvial clay, together with various bones of extinct species of animals, is considered by Carl Vogt to be of like antiquity with the Engis and Neanderthal skulls.[48]

CHAPTER IV.

PRE-GLACIAL EPOCHS.

The age immediately preceding the glacial, and consequently the post-tertiary, is known as the pliocene epoch, the last of the tertiary.

The tertiary period began with the close of the cretaceous. A map of the early tertiary period would represent parts of Maryland, Virginia, the

Carolinas, Georgia, the whole of Florida, the lower parts of Alabama, Mississippi, Texas, the whole of Louisiana, and the adjoining territory on both sides of the Mississippi, as far as Cairo, as covered with water. Also a great sea extending through Nebraska and the western part of Dacotah, and taking a north-westerly course until it emptied into the Pacific. In Europe, the great basin of Paris (excepting a zone of chalk), the greater part of Spain and Italy, the whole of Belgium, Holland, Prussia, Switzerland, Hungary, Wallachia, and northern Russia, as one vast sheet of water. England and France were connected by a band of rocks.

About the middle of the tertiary, a tropical climate and tropical fauna and flora spread over the whole of Europe. Palms, cedars, laurels, and cinnamon trees flourished in the valleys of Switzerland, and more than thirty different species of oak adorned the forests of that time.

In Europe, in the eocene, there have been found thirty species of crocodiles; many species of snakes, one twenty feet long; a dozen species of birds; tapirs (Palaeothere and Lophiodon), two species of hogs, some ruminants and rodents.

In the miocene, among Pachyderms may be mentioned the mastodon, elephant, dinothere (an elephantine animal), rhinoceros, hog, horse, tapir, and hippopotamus; among Carnivores, the machairodus, hyena, lion, and dog; among Ruminants, the camel, deer, and antelope. There were monkeys, and many other animals.

In the pliocene, besides those enumerated, are found the bear, hare, and other animals.

In the tertiary beds of America have been found mastodons, elephants, rhinoceroses, deer, camels, foxes, wolves, horses, whales, and other mammalia.

Owing to the great lapse of time it cannot be expected that many traces of man will be discovered in this early period.

Upon theoretical grounds Lyell thought it very probable that man lived in the pliocene; but in relation to miocene time, he says, "Had some other rational being, representing man, then flourished, some signs of his existence could hardly have escaped unnoticed, in the shape of implements of stone or metal, more frequent and more durable than the osseous remains of any of the mammalia."[49] Sir J. Lubbock, while admitting the existence of man in the pliocene, goes farther and says, "If man constitutes a separate family of mammalia, as he does in the opinion of the highest authorities, then, according to all palaeontological analogies, he must have had representatives in miocene times. We need not, however, expect to find the proofs in Europe; our nearest relatives in the animal kingdom are confined to hot, almost to tropical climates, and it is in such countries that we are most likely to find the earliest traces of the human race."[50] Alfred R. Wallace out-distances any of his cotemporaries, for he says, "We are enabled to place the origin of man at a much more remote geological epoch than has yet been thought possible. He may even have lived in the miocene or eocene period, when not a single mammal was identical in form with any existing species."[51]

Some of the older and some of the recent discoveries of geologists have settled the question of tertiary man; and the "signs of his existence," in the "shape of implements of stone," as demanded by Lyell, have been furnished.

Man in the Pliocene.--It has already been intimated that the evidences of man are but few in this early epoch. The first example, in the following list, borders closely on the glacial, but far enough removed as to be referred to the pliocene.

In the construction of a canal between Stockholm and Gothenburg it was necessary to cut through one of those hills called osars, or erratic blocks, which were deposited by the drift-ice during the glacial epoch. Beneath an immense accumulation of osars, with shells and sand, there was discovered in the deepest layer of subsoil, at a depth of about sixty feet, a circular mass of stones, forming a hearth, in the middle of which there were wood-coals. No other hand than that of man could have performed the work.[52]

In the pliocene beds in the neighborhood of the town of Savonia in Liguria, M. A. Issel found several bones which presented all the physical signs of very high antiquity. Dr. Buchner is of the opinion that before these bones can be employed as satisfactory evidence they must have a more accurate test by scientific authorities.[53]

In the upper pliocene beds at St. Prest (France), M. Desnoyers found traces of human action on the bones of animals belonging to the tertiary. These fractures are analogous to those of human action observed on bones from the glacial period, and identical with those made by northern tribes of the present day, on the skulls of ruminants. The marked bones found were those of the Southern elephant (E. meridionalis), rhinoceros (R. leptorinus), hippopotamus major, several species of deer, and two of the ox. Carl Vogt states that this discovery is not only genuine, but also, the formation in which the bones were found is decidedly tertiary. It is further characterized by the presence of the southern elephant (E. meridionalis). As this elephant became extinct before the glacial age, the bones consequently precede the glacial, and the age of the cave-bear, the mammoth, and tichorrhine rhinoceros. The eminent French naturalist, Quatrefages, confirms the testimony of Desnoyers.[54]

The conclusions of Desnoyers are confirmed beyond a doubt by the more recent discoveries of Abbe Bourgeois. In the same tertiary strata of St. Prest, in which were found the marked or fractured bones, Bourgeois discovered worked flints, including flakes, awls, and scrapers.[55]

A human skull, belonging to the pliocene, was found by James Matson, at Altaville, in Calaveras county, California, at a depth of one hundred and thirty feet, under five beds of gravel separated by five layers of lava, associated with the bones of an extinct rhinoceros, camel, and horse. The base of the skull is imbedded in a mass of bone-breccia and small pebbles of volcanic rock. The shape of the skull resembles that of the Digger Indians, and is of remarkable thickness.[56]

Man in the Miocene.[57]--M. Bourgeois has found, in a stratum of miocene near Pontlevoy, numerous worked flints, and other flints which have been subjected to the action of heat. These works of man were associated with the remains of the acerotherium (an extinct species allied to the rhinoceros), and beneath five distinct beds, one of which contained the rolled bones of rhinoceros, mastodon, and dinotherium.[58]

M. Tardy found a flint-flake of undoubted workmanship in the miocene beds of Aurillac (Auvergne), together with the remains of dinotherium giganteum, and machaerodus latidens.[59]

M. Bourgeois reports that Abbe Delaunay had found near Pouance (Maine-et-Loire), fossil bones of a halitherium (an herbivorous cetacean of the miocene), with evident signs of having been operated upon by cutting instruments.[60]

In the miocene gravel beds of Colorado and Wyoming territories, chert-flakes, hammers, chisels, knives, and wrought shells have been found.[61]

Eocene.--As yet geologists have failed to discover any traces of man in the Eocene epoch.

CHAPTER V.

CONDITION OF MAN IN THE EARLIEST TIMES.

Of the first appearance of man on the globe there is no precise knowledge. His origin is a mystery. The place of his birth is generally supposed to be in Central Asia. There the geologist looks with a longing eye, and hopes ultimately to unravel, not only the hidden mystery of the birth-place of his race, but also, how or through what natural process he sprang into existence.

If the miocene be the earliest point in his history, and Central Asia the place of his nativity, then he was ushered upon the scene of life during the period of, and surrounded by, the numerous fauna of India, At this time her mammalia included, besides the quadrumana, elephant (seven species), mastodon (three species), rhinoceros (five species), horse (three species), hippopotamus (four to seven species), hog (three species), camel, giraffe, sivatherium (an elephantine stag, having four horns and supposed to have had the bulk of an elephant and greater height), antelope, musk-deer, sheep, ox (several species), dinotherium, porcupine, species of hyena, lion, and many others.

It cannot be presumed that man's intellectual faculties were ordinarily developed, as it would not be natural to suppose he was superior to that of later times. Judging from the remains of later times, man could have been but very little removed from the brute. It is natural to suppose that at first he had no fire, no weapons of offence or defence. His food must have been the herbs, roots, and the fruits of the tree, possibly with an occasional morsel of raw meat. His pillow was a stone, his retreat a cave or the boughs of a wide-spreading tree, and his clothing a natural coat of hair.

In the presence of the fierce beasts, man's domain might seem to be of short duration. Providence has ordered all things wisely. Placed low in the scale of life--brutal, selfish, prowling, yet cautious--man, by the very force of circumstances, was to develop gradually the powers of his mind. With the elephant and the mastodon he could not cope nor would they molest him. To the fierce carnivora he might fall a prey. From these he could flee, and find a shelter in the tops of the trees or some secure fastness of the earth. Learning his own strength by experience, he would venture forth on excursions, and meet face to face his deadly foe. For self-defence he discovered, probably by accident, that a club was a powerful weapon with which to beat back his fierce opponent. Gradually he came to learn that a sharp flint driven into the end of a club was a safer and more deadly weapon. With this he could withstand an unequal contest.

The mode of life, together with the trials of his strength, developed his muscular system. His muscles became large and tough, and his bones thick and heavy. The earliest type of man is generally supposed to be dolichocephalic, or long-headed. The walls of the skull were thick, and the crown low. He was of ordinary stature, but built for action, and of great power. His make-up was the result of his surroundings.

His advancement was very slow. Throughout the entire length of the miocene and pliocene epochs it is not traceable. There was no revolution in his mind; one step in advance would have been a mighty leap. Nor could it be expected that there should be rapid progress. The mind was brutal; and all the instincts sensual. But there was pending a mighty change. The tropical climate should change into a winter of snow and ice. Man should feel it, and be benefited by the new danger. His sluggish mind should be quickened, and the inventive genius should be called into action. The sun no longer could give its heat. The forests grew cold, the chilling winds swept over the plains, and the retreat in the cave was damp and forbidding. The wild beasts were either dying of cold, or else becoming clothed with thick, long hair, and retreating before the accumulating snow. Man earnestly looked about him.

He suffered greatly, and his numbers grew less. Fire had been produced. How, no one can tell; possibly by accident. He now became more careful of the fire, and with brand in hand he went from place to place kindling the fires at the various resting-places. Nor was this sufficient. His ingenuity was taxed to its greatest extent. Colder and colder grew the winds. The snow, coming in great flakes, was soon consolidated, and became as ice. The body could not be kept warm. Clothing must be had, and this must be furnished by the wild beasts. Their hides must assist in protecting the life of man. The stiffened, frozen animals would not alone furnish sufficient covering. Knives must be invented. From the flint rude knives were fashioned, by means of which the skins were removed and transferred to the bodies of men. But the long winter continuing, the lives of the living animals must be forfeited, both for the flesh and and the skins. Rude, almost shapeless arrow-heads were produced. Wood must be had with which to warm and cook, and rude rafts formed, by means of which the swelling rivers might be crossed. Then those stone hatchets of the Somme were shaped, and answered the purpose.

Man was at last prepared to face the rigors of winter, the perils of ice, and secure himself against starvation. Not content with his conflicts with nature, his brutal passion is aroused against his fellows. Death-dealing blows fall rapidly upon each other, the blood flows freely, the bones give way, and the weaker one has succumbed. There are fierce contentions over the common prey, and the strong impose upon the weak. True to his instinct, he is gregarious. He lives in communities; and the more daring--the hunters--having their common places of meeting, fashion their weapons, and vie with each other in feats of prowess.

During the glacial epoch the condition of man must have remained unchanged, after he had supplied himself with rude stone weapons. His time was spent, for the most part, in self-preservation. He was retreating before, yet bounding over, the frozen flood in pursuit of game. This experience must ultimately tell for good. When the glaciers began to recede, man followed closely, and forgot not the value of those stone weapons which had secured food for himself. They served against the cave-bear, cave-hyena, cave-lion, and would be of great service in the ages yet to come. By a little remodelling they could be used to greater advantage; and this change of shape was accomplished, and other uses of flint were made known.

Man's form, aspect, and true position are comprehended by the relics of the glacial age. The human bones tell a tale which any anatomist may read, and even one not well skilled in the art. The primitive type is no mystery, and those fossil bones tell of the terrific strifes of by-gone times.

The Neanderthal man has already been described. Its structure is animal. Its history agrees with the generally received idea of primitive man as conceived by the geologist. The illustration (frontispiece) presents him bestial and ape-like. A powerful organization, and well adapted to those times. His bones tell of fearful conflicts. He lived to an old age, as the traces of every suture are effaced. His skull was very thick. The strong, prominent superciliary arches denote large perceptives, making him watchful and always on the alert. Those bones tell of a terrible conflict. The left arm was broken; who knows but in a contest with the great cave-bear. He survived the contest and lived to see that arm dwindle and become almost useless. Over the right eye he received a blow, from some source, so great as to carry away a portion of the bone. The claw of a cave-bear, or a flint weapon in the hand of one of his race, may have produced that fracture. Still he lived, and the wound healed. All this tells of his strength and hardihood. It gives an inside view of the wonderful hardships and vicissitudes of primeval man.

The Engis skull belongs to the same type, though less bestial. Possibly this individual did not enter upon the chase, and engage in the manly pursuits of those times. He may have been an adviser or a dandy; or, his ingenuity may have led him to the vocation of fashioning weapons and implements from the flint.

In the time of the Engis man there were large as well as short, heavy-set men. In the same cavern there was found a clavicle belonging to a young person who must have been of great stature.

The jaws of La Naulette and Moulin-Quignon display a great tendency to animal structure, and confirm the impressions as given of the primitive condition of man during the glacial and pre-glacial ages.

CHAPTER VI.

INTER-GLACIAL EPOCH.

The glaciers have departed. Summer comes again. The forests bloom and the wild beast roams about. Many species withstood the long siege of cold; others perished; still others followed the ice as it retreated, preferring the cold to the coming heat. The floods had abated and man spread himself over the different tracts blooming with flowers and radiant with earthly splendors.

The evidences of man's existence during this period are numerous, consisting in works of art and fossil remains. Only a few examples are given, as not many will be required to present the evidence and show man's condition.

The hyena-den at Wokey Hole, explored by Mr. Dawkins, affords specimens of the works of man. When discovered this den was filled to the roof with debris. Under this rubbish was found several layers of the excrement of the cave-hyena (H. spelaea), each of which indicates an old floor and a separate period of occupation.

The implements were under these layers of excrement, showing that the cave had been occupied by the hyenas after the time of the savages. These implements had not been disturbed by the action of water. In the bone earth along with the remains of the cave-hyena were found those of the mammoth, Siberian rhinoceros, (R. tichorrhinus), gigantic ox (Bos primigenius), gigantic Irish deer (Megaceros Hibernicus), reindeer, cave-bear, cave-lion (Felis spelaea), wolf (Canis lupus), fox (Canis vulpes), and the teeth and bones of the horse in great numbers. Intermixed with these bones were chipped flints, a bleached flint weapon of the spear-head Amiens type, and arrow-heads made of bone.

[Illustration: FIG. 11. IDEAL SCENE IN THE POST-TERTIARY.

On the right is shown the megatherium. This animal belonged to the sloth tribe, and was a native of South America. It exceeded in size the largest rhinocerous, and the length of its skeleton sometimes attained eighteen feet. In front, near the centre, is the glyptodon another South American animal of the armadillo tribe. The length of its shell, along the curve, was five feet, and the total length of the animal, nine feet. Just back of the glypodon, and holding on to a tree, is the mylodon, belonging to both North and South

America, one species of which was much larger than the western buffalo. On the left, and in the rear, is the mastodon, the remains of which are found in both North and South America, though of different species. While this scene does not represent the animals with which we are dealing, yet the general features give an idea of those with which we are interested.]

[Illustration: FIG. 12. SECTION OF THE SEPULCHRAL GROTTO, IN THE HILL OF FAJOLES, AURIGNAC.

a. Vault in which the seventeen human skeletons were found.

b. Layer of made ground, two feet thick, inside the grotto in which a few human bones, with entire bones of extinct and living species of animals, and many works of art, were imbedded.

c. Layers of ashes and charcoal eight inches thick, containing broken, burned, and gnawed bones of extinct and living mammalia, also hearth-stones and works of art; no human bones.

d. Deposit with similar contents; also a few scattered cinders.

e. Talus of rubbish washed down from the hill above.

f, g. Slab of rock which closed the vault.

i, f. Rabbit-burrow.

h, k. Original terrace.

N. Nummulitic limestone.]

In the cavern of Maccagnone, in Sicily, there were found ashes and rude flint implements in a breccia containing the bones of the elephant (E. antiquus), hyena, a large bear, lion, (probably F. spelaea), and large numbers of bones belonging to the hippopotamus. The concrete of ashes had once filled the cavern, and a large piece of bone breccia was still cemented to the roof.

The vast number of hippopotamuses implies that the physical condition of the country was different from what it is at present. The bone breccia cemented to the roof, and coated with stalagmite, testifies that the cave, at some time since the formation of the breccia, has been washed out. The exact time of the formation of this breccia cannot be given, but, in all probability, not long after the extinction of the cave-bear, if not before.

The cave or grotto of Aurignac, in which the seventeen human skeletons were found, was carefully examined by Lartet eight years after its discovery. The recess was formed in nummulitic limestone. In front of the grotto, and next to the limestone (c, Fig. 12) was a layer of ashes and charcoal, eight inches thick, containing hearth-stones, works of art, and broken, burned, and gnawed bones of extinct and recent mammalia. Immediately above this layer (d) was another, of made ground, two feet thick, extending into the grotto; and its contents similar to the other, save that within the grotto were found a few human bones. The grotto was closed by a slab, and the made earth without was covered by a talus of rubbish (e), washed down from the hill above.

In these layers were found not less than one hundred flint instruments, consisting of knives, projectiles, sling-stones, chips, and a stone made for the purpose of modelling the flints. The bone implements were barbless arrows, a well-shaped and sharply pointed bodkin made of the horn of the roe-deer, and other tools made of reindeer horn. Besides these there were found eighteen small round and flat plates, of a white shelly substance, made of some species of cockle (cardium), pierced through the middle; also the tusk of a young cave-bear, the crown of which had been carved in imitation of the head of a bird.

The following is a list of the different species found in the layers, together with the approximate number of individuals belonging to each:

I.--CARNIVORA.

Number of Individuals. 1. Cave Bear (U. Spelaeus) 5-6 2. Brown Bear (U. arctos) 1 3. Badger (Meles taxus) 1-2 4. Polecat (Putorius vulgaris) 1 5. Cave Lion (Felis spelaea) 1 6. Wild Cat (Felis Catus ferus) 1 7. Hyena (H. spelaea) 5-6 8. Wolf (Canis lupus) 3 9. Fox (C. vulpes) 18-20

II.--HERBIVORA.

1. Mammoth (E. primigenius) Two molars and an astragalus. 2. Rhinoceros (R. tichorrhinus) 1 3. Horse (Equus caballus) 12-15 4. Ass (E. asinus) 1 5. Boar (Sus scrofa) Two incisors. 6. Stag (Cervus elephas) 1 7. Gigantic Irish Deer (Megaceros Hibernicus) 1 8. Roebuck (C. capreolus) 3-4 9. Reindeer (C. tarandus) 10-12 10. Aurochs (Bison Europaeus) 12-15

The bones on the outside of the grotto were found to be split open, as if for the extraction of the marrow, and many of them burned. The spongy parts were wanting, having been gnawed off by the hyenas.

M. Lartet came to the conclusion that this grotto was a place of sepulchre, and the broken or split bones were the remnants of the funeral feasts. This he argued from the fact that the bones within the grotto were not split, broken or gnawed, save the astragalus of the mammoth. This meat was placed in the grotto, probably as an offering to the dead. The bones without the cave were scraped, and while the men were yet engaged in the funeral feast, the hyenas prowled about the spot, and at the close of the banquet, devoured the flesh that remained. The slab in front of the cave debarred their entrance, and consequently the bones and human remains within were left untouched.

The observations made by M. Cartailhac, in 1870, lead to different conclusions. On close inspection, he discovered a difference in the color of the walls of the cave, indicating that the lower deposit was of a yellow color, and the next above of a much lighter tint. In the crevices of the lower he found a tooth of the rhinoceros, one of the reindeer, and some fractured bones of the cave-bear. In the higher deposit occurred some small bones of living animals and of man, and a fragment of pottery. From these evidences, M. Cartailhac inferred that the lower deposits of the grotto corresponded with that outside of it, and the layer containing human bones was formed at a subsequent time.

That this grotto was a place of resort at a very early period is proven from the numerous remains of the cave-bear. This animal was one of the first of those great post-tertiary mammalia to become extinct. The exact position of the remains of the reindeer is not given. If its bones were intermixed with the others and found in the lowest as well as the other layers, it would indicate that the climate was not very warm during the deposit of the layers, but to have been similar to that of Switzerland of the present day. The probability is, the reindeer bones did not occur in the lowest layer, and hence that layer was formed during the tropical climate, and the reindeer bones and human skeletons were consigned to the grotto about the close of the inter-glacial, or beginning of the reindeer epoch.

The fossil man of Denise, taken from an old volcanic tuff, must be assigned to this period, since there have been found, in similar blocks of tuff in the same region, the remains of the cave-hyena and hippopotamus major. This fossil man consists of a frontal part of the skull, the upper jaw, with teeth, belonging to both an adult and young individual; a radius, some lumbar vertebrae, and some metatarsal bones. The tuff is light and porous, and none of the bones penetrate into the more compact rock.

In the rubbish heap, or reindeer station, at the source of the Schusse, there were discovered more than six hundred split flints, with a quantity of partly worked antlers and bones of the reindeer. The bones were so numerous that Mr. Oscar Fraas was enabled to put together a complete skeleton of the reindeer which is now preserved in the museum of Stuttgart. Most of the bones were split open for the purpose of extracting the marrow. There were numerous remains of fishes, and a fish-hook manufactured from reindeer horn. There were also the bones of other animals, such as the glutton, arctic fox, and other animals now living in high northern latitudes.

Speaking of this station, Dr. Buchner says, "Not only the careful investigations of the geognostic conditions of the place, but also the flora of the time (for remains of mosses were found which now live only in the extreme north), leave no doubt that the reindeer station on the Schusse belongs to the glacial epoch, or that it probably belongs exactly to the interval between the two glacial epochs which in all probability Switzerland has experienced. Mr. E. Desor declared this deposit to be the terminal moraine of the Rhine-glacier, which was formerly very large. Moreover, according to him, this discovery is particularly remarkable, because it is the first example of a station of the reindeer-men in a free and open deposit, their remains having hitherto been found only in caves."[62]

From the remarks of Dr. Buchner, the great number of bones of the reindeer, and some show of advancement in the arts, it may be safe to conclude that this station belongs to the close of the inter-glacial.

CHAPTER VII.

CONDITION OF MAN IN THE INTER-GLACIAL.

The Inter-Glacial period continued a great length of time, covering many thousands of years.

Man is an improvable being, and some advancement may be expected in his condition. His mode of life, and continued conflicts with the fierce wild beasts, would tax his every device. Necessity compelled him to be inventive. The limited, bestial mind which he possessed, could not grapple with the higher problems of existence. United efforts and fortified places were beyond his thoughts. Those old axes of flint were great objects to his mind, and one step beyond them was a great stride in progress. That they developed but little cannot be wondered at, not only from their low type, but also from the knowledge that even in the era of history there are nations whose civilization has become fixed and stereotyped for ages; others, who, instead of advancing, have been retrograding.

The impulse given by the rigors of glacial times acted beneficially throughout this period. The rude axes and flints were retained, but improvements were made in utilizing the bones and horns of animals. Out of these, bodkins, fish-hooks, and arrow-heads were made. The teeth of wild animals were perforated, and, along with corals and shells, were used for ornaments. The caverns, used as dwelling-places, being destitute of water, this necessary of life was supplied and carried thither in rude vessels made of clay and dried in the sun. The arrows, flint knives, and axes were used for killing and skinning the animals, splitting the bones containing the marrow, shaping the bone implements, felling trees, and stripping the bark, which was used at times for clothing, after having been softened by beating. He commenced the art of engraving, as is witnessed by a sketch of the great cave-bear wrought on a curious stone found in the cave of Massat (Ariege), the bird's head formed from the bone of a cave-bear, at Aurignac, and other examples. The lower jaw-bones of the cave-bear and cave-lion, in the shape of hoes, used for digging roots, were found in the caves of Lherm and in Bouicheta. He made hearth-stones, and on them cooked his food. That he paid honors to the dead, and sheltered them from the ravages of beasts of prey, at present, must remain an open question. If he did, it might seem to imply that he had a religious nature. But when it is considered that he was very low in the scale of existence, it may be inferred that this was done, if done at all, to propitiate an evil genius. Or it may be a faint idea of a ghost state and that these feasts were made to dissuade the ghost from molesting him. That they had a conception of a Supreme Ruler, or a number of gods who ruled for the good of man, would be too preposterous to believe.

Professor Denton has given a description of primeval time which, by a little change, would represent inter-glacial times: "The seasons are fairly established; and spring follows winter, and fall summer, as now; though the summer is longer and warmer than we are accustomed to see in those countries at the present time, and the winters colder. The country is covered with dense forests, through which ramble mighty elephants in herds, with immense curved tusks, coats of long, shaggy hair, and flowing manes.... Shuffling along comes the great cave-bear from his rocky den--as large as a horse: fierce, shaggy, conscious of his strength, he fears no adversary. Crouched by a bubbling spring lies the cave-tiger (Felis spelaea); and, as the wild cattle come down to drink, he leaps upon the back of one, and a terrible combat ensues. It is as large as an elephant, and its horns of enormous size; and even cave-tigers could not always master such cattle as they.

"Are these the highest forms of life that the country contains? What being is that sitting on yon fallen tree? His long arms are in front of his hairy body, and his hands between his knees; while his long legs are dangling down. His complexion is darker than an Indian's; his beard short, and like the hair of his body; the unkempt hair of his head is bushy and thick; his eyebrows are short and crisp; and with his sloping forehead and brutal countenance, he seems like the caricature of a man, rather than an actual human being.

"Beneath the shade of a spreading chestnut we may behold a group--one old man ... and women and children, lounging and lying upon the ground. How dirty! What forbidding countenances!--more like furies than women. One young man, with a stone axe, is separating the bark from a neighboring tree. Others, agile as monkeys, are climbing the trees, and passing from branch to branch, as they gather the wild fruit that abounds on every side. Some are catching fish in the shallows of the river, and yell with triumph as they hold their captives by the gills, dragging them to the shore."[63]

They have improved their language, and instead of the rude signs and undistinguishable sounds of the glacial, may now be heard short, but occasional sentences, which were the forerunners of the polished tongues of modern Europe.

CHAPTER VIII.

REINDEER EPOCH.

The glaciers, to a limited extent, have again advanced. The gigantic animals of the past age have either disappeared or are fast becoming extinct. The great cave-bear, cave-lion, cave-hyena, mammoth, and woolly-haired rhinoceros have almost become extinct. They have given way to a less fierce and less gigantic fauna. The advance of the glaciers is announced by the numerous herds of reindeer which are overrunning the forests of Western Europe, and extending as far south as the Pyrenees. In the forests there now existed the horse, bison, wild bull (Bos primigenius), musk-ox, elk, deer, chamois, ibex, beaver, hamster-rat, lemming, and many others. These animals were capable of withstanding and flourishing in a rigorous climate. When the glaciers were again broken up and the climate became warmer, the reindeer, musk-ox, elk, chamois, wild-goat, hamster-rat, and lemming retired to the high northern latitudes in close proximity to the snow, or else to the lofty summits of great mountain-chains.

The evidences of the antiquity of the reindeer epoch, and that it immediately followed the inter-glacial, are numerous. The vast number of the reindeer bones and horns attest to a distinct epoch, and by the remains of arctic animals, as well as the traces of glaciers, the climate must have been unlike that of the present time. The remains of the mammoth, cave-bear, and cave-lion, would not only connect this period with the inter-glacial, but also prove that a few stragglers continued to exist, at least for a short period, after the reindeer epoch had begun. That this epoch was earlier than the Swiss lake-villages, or Danish shell mounds, may be shown by the weapons or implements which point to a more primitive people, the absence of the remains of the dog, and, also, by the absence of the remains of the reindeer in the shell-mounds.

There are no means, yet discovered, by which it can be told how long this epoch lasted. It lasted a sufficient length of time to permit the reindeer to increase greatly its species.

Evidences of the Existence of Man.--M. Christy and M. Lartet examined in conjunction the caves of Central and Southern France. Those which have been most carefully examined are ten in number, and belong to the Department of Dordogne. At Perigord there seems to have been quite a settlement, judging by the number of caves and stations, the principal ones being Les Eyzies, La Madeleine, Laugerie-Haute, and Laugerie-Basse.

At Les Eyzies there were found a flint bodkin and a bone needle used for sewing, a barbed arrow made of reindeer horn and still fixed in a bone, a flint whistle made from the first joint of the foot of the reindeer, and two slabs of schist, on both of which were scratched animal forms, but deficient in any special characteristic.

At La Madeleine there were found a geode very large and very thick, which, it is supposed, was used for a cooking vessel, as one side of it had been subjected to fire; an engraving of a reindeer on the horn of that animal; on another horn the carved outlines of two fishes, one on either side; a representation of an ibex on the palm of a horn; on another, a very curious group, consisting of an eel, a human figure, and two horses' heads. A slab of ivory, broken into five pieces, had an outline sketch of the mammoth (Fig. 13). This was so accurately drawn that the small eye, curved tusks, huge trunk, and the abundant mane, could readily be distinguished. There was also found, on an arrow-head, the figure of a tadpole.

There were workshops at Laugerie-Haute and Laugerie-Basse, where weapons and utensils were manufactured; and they are noted for the abundance of instruments made of reindeer horn. Among the works of art found at the latter station may be mentioned, the stiletto, needle, spoon made in the shape of rods tapering off at one end and hollow in the middle, staff of authority, whistle, and harpoon, all from the horn of the reindeer. On the head of a staff of authority is carved a mammoth's head; there is a representation of the hind-quarters of some herbivorous animal, sketched out with a bold and practiced touch; an animal's head, with ears laid back, and of considerable length, is carved on a round shaft of reindeer horn. It cannot be determined for what purpose this shaft was intended, but as the other end was pointed, and provided with a lateral hook, it may have been the harpoon of some chief. On a slab of slate was drawn, in outline, a reindeer fight. On a fragment of a spear-head there is a series of human hands, provided with four fingers only, and represented in demi-relief. The delineations of fish are principally on wands of authority--on one of which is a series following one another.

[Illustration: FIG. 13. SKETCH OF A MAMMOTH, GRAVEN ON A SLAB OF IVORY FROM LA MADELEINE.]

The cave and rock shelters of Bruniquel (Tarn-et-Garonne) have been carefully examined by competent explorers. These relics are so numerous that M. de Lastic, the proprietor of the cavern, sold to the agent of the British Museum fifteen hundred specimens, of every description, which had been found on his property. In the cave there were found, engraved on a bone, a perfectly recognizable horse's head and the head of a reindeer, and daggers made of ivory and bone, on which were representations of the above-mentioned animals. The engravings are mostly on the horn of the reindeer. The cave has also furnished two almost perfect human skulls, and two half-jaw bones which resemble the Moulin-Quignon.

The rock-shelters are overhanging rocks, under the projections of which man found a shelter and built his rude dwellings of boughs and sticks. In these shelters have been found fire-hearths, fish-hooks made of splinters of bone, saws made of flint, a complete sketch of the mammoth engraved on reindeer horn, the hilt of a dagger carved in the shape of a reindeer, the cave-lion, engraved with great clearness, on a fragment of a staff of authority, and two daggers made of ivory.

In the excavations which were made in the rock-shelters, was found a quantity of human bones, including two skulls--one of an old man, the other that of an adult.

The cave of Gourdan (Haute-Garonne) contained the largest collection of implements of bone and horn ever discovered. The stones and reindeer horns are carved with great care, and indicate a high degree of artistic taste. There are sketches made of the reindeer, stag, chamois, goat, bison, horse, wolf, boar, monkey, badger, antelope, fishes, and birds, and also the representations of some plants. In the lowest layer of the soil the most perfect works occur, and they grow less as the surface is approached. Several of those implements called "batons of command" occurred, ornamented with animals' heads. On the rib of a horse was carved an antelope, and on the bone of a bird various figures--plants, reindeer, and a fish. This cave was made the subject of a report by M. Piette before the Paris Anthropological Society.

[Illustration: FIG. 14. THE FOSSIL MAN OF MENTONE.]

The fossil man of Mentone, found in a grotto of Mentone, a village near Nice, for some time past has produced much comment among scientists. The skeleton was discovered in undisturbed earth; at a depth of twenty-one feet. The cause of the discussion is that the skeleton is accompanied by a multiplicity of bone-tools, needles, chisels, a baton of command, a necklace, various species of the deer, indicating the reindeer epoch, but surrounded also by the remains of the cave-bear, cave-hyena, and woolly-haired rhinoceros. Dr. Garrigou arrives at the conclusion that this cave was first inhabited by men of the preceding epoch, or inter-glacial, and during the reindeer epoch was used as a place of burial.[64] The attitude of the skeleton was that of repose (see Fig. 14). It was stained by oxide of iron. The tibiae, or shin-bones, present a noticeable feature by being more flattened than in the European of the present time.

In the same neighborhood there have more recently been discovered, in different caves, four other human skeletons. They were all stained with oxide of iron, and two of them surrounded with pierced sea-shells, teeth of the stag, constituting the remains of necklaces and bracelets. With one skeleton, which belonged to a large individual, were discovered implements of stone and bone, tooth of a cave-bear, bones of other animals, and shells of edible marine mollusks. The other two skeletons were those of children, and not accompanied by either implements or ornaments.

The other bone caves of France, which have afforded much valuable information, and belonging to this epoch, are: La Gorge d'Enfer, Liveyre, Pey de l'Aze, Combe-Granal, Le Moustier and Badegoule (Dordogne), cave of Bize (Aude), cave of La Vache (Ariege), cave of Savigne (Vienne), grottos of La Balme and Bethenas, in Dauphine, the settlement of Solutre, the cave of Lourdes (Hautes-Pyrenees), and the cave of Espalungue (Basses-Pyrenees)-- the last two date back to the most ancient period of the reindeer epoch.

The principal objects found in these caves, and the rock-shelters are worked flakes, scrapers, cores, awls, lance-heads, cutters, hammers, and mortar-stones. These works, though unpolished, are but little ruder than those of the Esquimaux or the North American Indian.

Belgian Caverns.--Under the auspices of the Belgian government M. Edward Dupont examined more than twenty caves on the banks of the Lesse, in the province of Namur. Among these were four, in which occurred numerous traces of the reindeer-man, namely, Trou du Frontal, Trou Rosette, Trou des Nutons, and Trou de Chaleux.

The cavern Trou de Frontal was a place of burial, and similar to the cave of Aurignac. The mouth of the cave was closed by a slab of sandstone, and within were the remains of fourteen human beings belonging to persons of various ages, and some of them to infants scarcely a year old. In front of the cave was an esplanade, where were celebrated the funeral feasts, and which was marked by hearth-stone, traces of fire, flint-knives, bones of animals, shells, etc. The human bones were intermixed with a considerable number of the bones of the reindeer and other animals, as well as the different kinds of implements. Among the remains were two perfect human skulls, in a good state of preservation. The bones were discovered in a state of great confusion, which M. Dupont thinks was caused by the disturbance of water. Sir John Lubbock regards the disturbance of the bones as due to foxes and badgers.[65]

Immediately above this cave is the Trou Rosette, in which the bones of three persons were found, mingled with those of the reindeer and beaver. It also contained fragments of a blackish kind of pottery, which were hollowed out in rough grooves and hardened by fire. Dupont is of opinion that the three men were crushed to death by masses of rock at the time of the inundation of the valley of the Lesse.

In the Trou des Nutons, situated one hundred and sixty-four feet above the Lesse, were found a great many bones of the reindeer, wild bull, and many other species. In the cave, indiscriminately mixed up with these bones, were one hundred and fifty worked reindeer horns, knuckle-bones of the goat, polished on both sides, a whistle made from the tibia of a goat, fragments of very coarse pottery, and fire-hearths.

[Illustration: FIG. 15. EARTHEN VASE, FOUND IN THE CAVE OF FURFOOZ, BELGIUM.]

The cave of Chaleux was buried by a mass of rubbish caused by the falling in of the roof, consequently preserving all its implements. There were found the split bones of mammals and the bones of birds and fishes. There was an immense number of objects, chiefly manufactured from reindeer horn, such as needles, arrow-heads, daggers, and hooks. Besides these, there were ornaments made of shells, pieces of slate with engraved figure, mathematical lines, remains of very coarse pottery, hearth-stones, ashes, charcoal, and last but not least, thirty thousand worked flints mingled with the broken bones. In the hearth, placed in the centre of the cave, was discovered a stone, with certain but unintelligible signs engraved upon it. M. Dupont also found about twenty pounds of the bones of the water-rat, either scorched or roasted.

In a cave at Furfooz, Dupont found an urn, or specimen of rough pottery (Fig. 15) intermingled with human bones. It was partly broken; by the care of M. Hauzeur it has been put together again.

France and Belgium are not alone in their monuments of the reindeer epoch, for settlements of this epoch have been discovered in Germany, Switzerland, and Poland.

In the cave of Thayngen, near Schaffhausen, Switzerland, have been discovered a few remains of the mammoth, rhinoceros, and cave-lion; the remains of two hundred and fifty reindeer, four hundred and thirty Alpine hares; also the remains of the brown bear, stag, elk, auroch, glutton, wolf, and several kinds of fox. The large bones invariably appeared in fragments, and the pebbles used for breaking them were found in the refuse. Among birds, the bones of the swan, grouse, and duck predominate. The implements consisted chiefly of needles, piercers, and arrow-heads made of the antlers of the reindeer. The art of engraving and carving was carried to quite a degree of perfection. The most notable of these objects is the delineation of a reindeer in the act of browsing, drawn on a piece of the horn of that animal.

Not far from Cracow (Poland), a cavern has been recently discovered and examined by Count Zawisza. In the upper part of the floor (four feet in depth), consisting of vegetable earth, mould, and debris, occurred ashes, flint implements, and the split bones of the cave-bear, reindeer, horse, elk, and other animals. Beneath this layer appeared the broken bones of the mammoth, an ornament of ivory, and the perforated teeth of the cave-bear, stag, elk, wolf, and fox. Two thousand flint implements were obtained; and from the frequent occurrence of flint the cave was used by the troglodytes, or cave-men, as a dwelling; and by the remains of the fauna, it must have been occupied during the inter-glacial, and at the beginning of the reindeer epoch.

CHAPTER IX.

MAN OF THE REINDEER EPOCH.

The Reindeer Epoch, approaching nearer the present age than those already enumerated, presents man under a more favorable aspect, and affords a better view of his traits of character and manner of living. Not only the sturdy climate spurs him to action, but a higher type is supplanting the original savages. The brachycephalic, or round-headed, has penetrated the recesses of that wild country and brought with him the art of making more perfect implements. This new type was of short stature, having small hands and feet. If Asia be the home of man, then from that country, advanced in civilization, came the vanguard who were destined to supplant their predecessors, tame the wild beasts, and conquer the forests. Representatives of this type are found in the Lapps and Fins. Between the two existing races--dolichocephalic and brachycephalic--there may have been a long and bitter strife. The former was large, stout, fearless, and cruel; the latter, small, hardy, and more intelligent. It was a conflict between brute force and intelligence. The more perfect weapons must have told fearfully against the rude axes and arrows of the dolichocephalic. It could not have been a war of extermination, for finally an intermixture took place, producing a medium, as may be judged from the exhumed skulls.

Dwellings.--As in the past ages, man continued to dwell, for the most part, in caves. If the cave was small, he occupied every portion; but if large, only that part near the opening was used. In the centre of this dwelling he made a hearth, out of stones sunk in the floor, and with the fire placed upon it, he cooked his meals and warmed his body. This mode of life did not always satisfy him, for he ventured out, and under the projection of an overhanging rock he built him a booth, or rude hut, out of boughs, and the poles of fallen timber. These dwellings, whether in caves or under the rocks, were near some stream.

Clothing.--The climate being cold, he probably ceased to use the inner bark of trees, and depended solely on the skins of animals. The skins were prepared by the flint scrapers, and then rendered supple by rubbing into them the brains and the marrow extracted from the skulls and long bones of the reindeer. These garments may have been artistically shaped, for they understood the art of sewing. With the bodkin they pierced the skin, and with the needle, end was held to end and side to side, and the same made permanent by the sinew of some animal.

Food.--These people were essentially hunters, and lived principally upon the reindeer, which they attacked with their spears and arrows. The horse, elk, ox, ibex, and the chamois, formed a considerable part of their food. The meat was cooked on the rough hearths, and the skull and the long bones were split open in order to extract the brains and marrow, which formed a delicious dish. To this they also added fish and, occasionally, certain birds, such as the heath-cock, swan, and owl. The chase did not always afford them sufficient food, and at times they were forced to subsist on the water-rat.

Enough evidence has been produced to show that these people were cannibals. Human finger-joints were discovered among the remains of cooking at Solutre in Maconnais. M. Issel found, at a point on the road from Genoa to Nice, some human bones which had been calcined, and were of a whitish color, light, and friable. The incrustations on their surface still contained small fragments of carbon, and some of them showed notches made by some sharp instrument. In one of the grottos of Northern Italy M. Costa de Beauregard found the small shin-bone of a child, which had been carefully emptied and cleansed. Professor Owen thinks he can recognize the trace of human teeth on some human skulls and children's bones found in Scotland, and promiscuously mixed with sculptured flints and the remains of pottery.

The Arts.--Man had not yet discovered the value of metal, but formed his instruments out of flint, bone, and the horn of the reindeer. The hatchet was but little used, and the principal weapons were the flint-knife, arrow-heads, and occasionally the lower jaw-bone of the cave-bear, with its pointed canine tooth. The articles of domestic use were rough pottery, knives, scrapers, saws, bodkins, needles, and other wrought implements. He had articles for ornamenting his person and pleasing his fancy, such as shells for beads, and the whistle for delighting his ear. The art of engraving was practised to a great extent, and so admirably did he execute his designs that, after the lapse of thousands of years, the figures are easily recognized.

The staff of authority would imply that there were certain individuals who were recognized as chiefs or leaders. Some system must have prevailed, for without it the manufactories at Laugerie-Basse and Laugerie-Haute could not have been carried on. In the first of these workshops the fabrications were almost wholly spear-heads, and in the second reindeer horn was used for the weapons and implements.

Traffic.--Commerce was begun. The inhabitants of Belgium sought their flints in that part of France now called Champagne. From the same locality they also brought back fossil shells, which were strung together and used for necklaces. There can be no doubt of this, as already fifty-four of these shells have been found at Chaleux, and they are not found naturally anywhere else than in Champagne.

Burial.--As in the previous epoch, the dead were consigned to the same kind of caves as were used for habitations, and the entombment was celebrated by the funeral-feast. These banquets afford no evidence of worship. Some have thought they not only saw signs of worship in the banquets, but also in some of the carvings. No idols have been found. That they should have no notion of a future state is not surprising, for Sir J. Lubbock has shown that there are tribes at the present time without this belief.[66]

M. Edward Dupont, in his report to the Belgian minister of the Interior, on the excavations carried on in the caves, has concisely but eloquently given a synopsis of man of the reindeer epoch, in the following language:

"The data obtained from the fossils of Chaleux, together with those which have been met with in the caves of Furfooz, present us with a striking picture of the primitive ages of mankind in Belgium. These ancient tribes, and all their customs, after having been buried in oblivion for thousands and thousands of years, are again vividly brought before our eyes; and, ... antiquity lives again in the relics of its former existence.

"We may almost fancy that we can see them in their dark and subterranean retreats, crouching round their hearths, and skilfully and patiently chipping out their flint instruments and shaping their reindeer-horn tools, in the midst of all the pestilential emanations arising from the various animal remains which their carelessness has allowed to remain in their dwellings. Skins of wild beasts are stripped of their hair, and, by the aid of flint needles, are converted into garments. In our mind's eye, we may see them engaged in the chase, and hunting wild animals--their only weapons being darts and spears, the fatal points of which are formed of nothing but a splinter of flint. Again, we are present at their feasts, in which, during the period when their hunting has been fortunate, a horse, a bear, or a reindeer, becomes the more noble substitute for the tainted flesh of the rat, their sole resource in the time of famine.

"Now, we see them trafficking with the tribes inhabiting the region now called France, and procuring the jet and fossil shells with which they love to adorn themselves, and the flint which is to them so precious a material. On one side they are picking up the fluor spar, the color of which is pleasing to their eyes; on the other, they are digging out the great slabs of sandstone which are to be placed as hearth-stones round their fire.

"But, alas! inauspicious days arrive." The roof of their principal cave falls in, burying their weapons and utensils, and forcing them "to fly and take up their abode in another spot. The ravages of death break in upon them.... They bear the corpse into its cavernous sepulchre; some weapons, an amulet, and perhaps an urn, form the whole of the funeral furniture. A slab of stone prevents the inroad of wild beasts. Then begins the funeral banquet, celebrated close by the abode of the dead; a fire is lighted, great animals are cut up, and portions of their smoking flesh are distributed to each. How strange the ceremonies that must then have taken place! ceremonies like those told us of the savages of the Indian and African solitudes. Imagination may easily depict the songs, the dances, and the invocations, but science is powerless to call them into life....

"But the end of this primitive age is at last come. Torrents of water break in upon the country. Its inhabitants, driven from their abodes, in vain take refuge on the lofty mountain summits. Death at last overtakes them, and a dark cavern is the tomb of the wretched beings, who, at Furfooz, were witnesses of this immense catastrophe."[67]

CHAPTER X.

NEOLITHIC EPOCH.

The Neolithic, or Epoch of Tamed Animals, is characterized by stone implements, polished or made smooth by a process of grinding and cutting, the greater development attained in the art of pottery, and by the presence of the bones of the domesticated animals. This age, in which no remains of the reindeer occur, immediately follows the reindeer epoch, and to it are referred in general all discoveries made in the so called alluvial soil, the most ancient remains of the so called Celts, the shell-heaps of Denmark, the tumuli or grave-mounds, the dolmens, the earlier Swiss pile-buildings, the Irish lake-dwellings, and some of the caves of France.

Caverns.--The caves belonging to this period, and explored by MM. Garrigou and Filhol, are those of the Pyrenees and the caves of Pradiers, Bedeilhac, Labart, Niaux, Ussat, and Fontanel. Some of these caverns have been used in earlier ages, as is shown by the remains of extinct mammals. The upper crust of the floors of the caves belong to this period, and in them are found the bones of the ox, stag, sheep, goat, antelope, chamois, wild boar, wolf, dog, fox, badger, hare, and horse, intermingled with the remains of hearths, also piercers, spear-heads, and arrow-heads, made of bone; hatchets, knives, scrapers made of flints, and various other substances, such as silicious schist, quartzite, leptinite, and serpentine stone. These implements were carefully wrought, and mostly polished.

The cave of Saint Jean d'Alcas (Aveyron), explored at different times by M. Cazalis de Fondace, was used as a place of sepulture. It was first examined about twenty-five years ago, and at that time five human skulls, in a good state of preservation, were found, but have been lost, as their importance was not then known. Intermingled with these bones were flint, jade, and serpentine implements, carved bones, remains of rough pottery, stone amulets, and the shells of shell-fish, but no remains of funeral banquets. At the mouth of the cave were two large flag-stones lying across one another. The most recent discoveries in the cave have furnished metallic substances, which would place it, as a habitation, to the last of the neolithic.

Danish Kjoekken-Moeddings, or Shell-Mounds, or kitchen-refuse heaps.-- The refuse heaps of Denmark were carefully examined by Professors Steenstrup, the naturalist, Forchammer, a geologist, and Worsaae, the archaeologist, commissioned by the Danish government, their reports being presented to the Academy of Sciences at Copenhagen.

They are found chiefly on the north coast of Denmark, and consist of the shells of edible mollusks, such as the oyster, cockle, mussel, and periwinkle. These deposits are from three to ten feet in thickness, from one hundred to two hundred and fifty feet in width, and sometimes as much as one thousand feet in length. In them are found weapons and other instruments of stone, horn, and bone; fragments of rough pottery, stone-wedges, knives, etc., in great abundance, accompanied with charcoal and ashes; no traces of coin, bronze, or iron, or domestic animals, except the dog. The bones of animals are very numerous, but no human bones have ever been discovered. Professor Steenstrup estimates that ninety-seven per cent. of the bones belong to the stag, the roe-deer, and the wild boar. The other remains are those of the urus (Bos primigenius), dog, fox, wolf, marten, wild-cat, hedgehog, bear (Ursus arctos), and the mouse, and the bones of birds and fishes. The auroch, musk ox, domestic ox, elk, hare, sheep, and domestic hog are absent.

The mollusca of these shell-mounds are of a size which are never obtained by the representatives of the same species now living on the Baltic. They are not more than one-half or even one-third the size. At the time of the formation of these mounds, the Baltic was a true sea, or an arm of the ocean, and these mollusks were taken from it. Now the Baltic has not the character of a true sea, but is merely brackish, and the oyster does not occur in the Baltic except at its entrance into the ocean.

These deposits have been found several miles inland, which would indicate that the sea had once covered the intervening space. On the western coast they have not been found, in consequence of their having possibly been swept away by the encroachments of the sea. They are also found on the adjacent islands.

These mounds are not peculiar alone to Denmark; for they are found in England, Scotland, France, and America.

Danish Peat Bogs.--The peat bogs of Denmark, so faithfully investigated by Professor Steenstrup, mark three periods of deposition. The most ancient is called the Scotch-Fir; the second, immediately above, the Oak, and the uppermost, the Beech. The peat is from ten to forty feet in thickness, and to form a layer from ten to twenty feet thick would require, according to Steenstrup, at least four thousand years, and perhaps even from three to four times that period.[68] These three epochs denote three periods of time. The lowest belongs to the neolithic, the middle to the bronze, and the last to the iron epoch. In the lowest, or Fir period, have been found worked flints and bones. Human bones have been found, which correspond with the bones taken from the tumuli of this epoch.

The Lake-Dwellings of Switzerland.--Dr. Ferdinand Keller and his associates have made known to the world the wonderful remains of villages situated in the lakes of Switzerland and other countries. The villages of Switzerland do not all belong to the same period, and they represent the neolithic, bronze, and iron epochs; but there was no hard line of demarcation between these three periods. These habitations are so numerous that more than two hundred settlements hare been discovered in Switzerland alone. Among the lakes furnishing these remains may be counted the Lake of Neuchatel (forty-six settlements); Lake Constance (thirty-two settlements); Lake of Geneva (twenty-four settlements); Lake of Bienne (twenty-one settlements); Lake of Morat (sixteen settlements); Lake of Zurich (three settlements); Lake of Pfaeffikon (six settlements); Lake of Sempach (six settlements); Lake of Moosseedorf (two settlements); Lake of Inkwyl (one settlement); Lake of Nussbaumen (one settlement); Lake Greiffensee (one settlement); Lake of

Zug (six settlements); Lake of Baldegg (five settlements), and others.

The habitations belonging to the neolithic are Lake Constance thirty, Neuchatel twelve, Geneva two settlements; one each at Morat, Bienne, Zurick, Pfaeffikon, Inkwyl, Moosseedorf, Nussbaumen, the settlement of Concise, the bridge Thiele, the peat-bog of Wauwyl, and others.

These dwellings were built near the shore, on piles of various kinds of wood, sharpened by tools and fire, and driven into the mud at the shallow bottom of the lake. In some of the settlements the piles were fastened by heaping stones around them. The piles were sometimes placed together, at others apart. The heads were brought to a level and then the platform beams were fastened upon them. This basis served for the foundation of the rude rectangular huts they erected. These piles are not now seen above the water, yet they are visible above the bottom of the lake. The number of piles in some of these settlements is as high as one hundred thousand, and the area occupied, not less than seventy thousand square yards. It has been estimated that the population of the Lake-villages during the neolithic was over thirty thousand.

The object of these dwellings was to protect the inhabitants from wild animals, the attacks of enemies, and for the ready obtaining of food by fishing. They were not only occupied by the inhabitants, but also by their herds and the stores of fodder.[69]

Robenhausen.--It is not necessary to go into an account of a number of these settlements to represent the neolithic epoch, for the settlement at Robenhausen (Lake Pfaeffikon) takes the first rank in giving the domestic arrangements of the ancient inhabitants. This settlement covered a space of nearly three acres, and one hundred thousand piles were used in the whole structure. Its form was an irregular quadrangle. It was about two thousand paces from the ancient western shore of the lake, and about three thousand from the shore in the opposite direction. With the last-named side there was a communication by means of a bridge, the piles of which are still visible. On this side were the gardens and pastures. The dwellers of this settlement were unfortunate, as their habitation was twice burned up, and each time, they rallied and rebuilt their huts. They remained a long time as would seem from the depth of the peat and the vast amount of relics found.

At a depth of eleven feet were found the earliest or most ancient relics; at ten and one-half feet, the remains of the first conflagration--charcoal, stone and bone implements, pottery, woven cloth, corn, apples, etc.; at seven and one-half feet, flooring, relics of the second settlement, and excrement of cows, sheep, and goats; at six and one half feet, remains of second conflagration--charcoal, stone and bone implements, pottery, woven cloth, corn, apples, etc.; at three and one-half feet, broken stones, flooring, and relics of the third settlement; at two and one half feet, stone celts, pottery, but no traces of fire. Above this was two feet of peat and one-half foot of mould.

Without going into detail, the objects found in these various beds are as follows: Made out of wood, are knives, ladles, plates, clubs of ash, in which is fixed a socket of stag's horn containing a stone celt, a boat made of a single trunk, twelve feet long, two and one-half feet wide, and five inches deep, flails for threshing out grain, bows notched at both ends, fishing implements, floats for the support of nets, suspension hooks, tubs, chisels, sandals, yokes made for carrying vessels, and a peculiar ornament. These implements were all made out of yew, maple, ash, fir, and the root of the hazel bush. Out of stag's horn--arrow-heads, daggers, piercing and scraping tools, implements for knitting and for agriculture. The implements of stone were polished, and of the usual form. The objects of clay were fragments of pottery, in the shape of urns, plates, and cups, in great abundance. There were also found spoons, and a perforated cone, supposed to have been used as a weight for the loom. Several crucibles or melting pots have been found, which were used for melting copper. The third building of this village was on the borderland between the stone and bronze ages.

The remains of animals found here and at Moosseedorf and Wauwyl, all of the neolithic, belong to the brown bear, badger, marten, pine-marten, polecat, wolf, fox, wild-cat, beaver, elk, urus, bison, stag, roe-deer, wild-boar, marsh-boar; the domestic animals were the boar, horse, ox, goat, sheep, and dog. The remains of the domestic hog are absent from all the pile works of this period, save the one at Wauwyl.

Among cereals (Robenhausen) were found several varieties of wheat and barley; fruits and berries--service-tree, dog-rose, elder, bilberry, and wayfaring tree; the nuts--hazel, beech, and water-chestnut; the oil-producing plants--opium, or garden poppy, and dogwood; the fibrous plants--flax; plants used for dying--weld; forest trees and shrubs--silver fir, juniper, yew, ash, and oak; water and marsh plants--lake scirpus, pondweeds, common hornwort, marsh bedstraw, buckbean, yellow waterlily, ivy-leaved crowfoot, and marsh pennywort.

Besides these there have been found many specimens of plaited and woven cloth; also ropes, cords, and a portion of a linseed cake.[70]

In the different settlements the same axes and knives abound, and are of small size. The arrow-heads and saws are an improvement on those of the preceding epoch. Among domestic implements, spindle-whorls of rude earthenware were abundant in some of the villages, and corn-crushers are occasionally met with from two to three inches in diameter. About five hundred implements of stone have been found at Wauwyl, consisting of axes, small flint arrow-heads, flint-flakes, corn-crushers, rude stones used as hammers, whetstones, and sling-stones.

As these Lake-Dwellings not only belong to the last of the neolithic, but extend beyond, they naturally have a place in the close of this period. M. Troyon says the dwellings of this period came suddenly to an "end by the irruption of a people provided with bronze implements. The lake-dwellings were burned by these new-comers, and the primitive inhabitants were slaughtered or driven back into remote places. This catastrophe affects chiefly the settlements of East Switzerland, which entirely disappeared, and also a number of those on the shore of the western lakes. Some few settlements, however--namely, those of the so-called transition period--are said not to have been destroyed by the new people till after the inhabitants had begun to make use of bronze implements."[71]

Dr. Keller takes exception to these views. He says there is no sudden leap from one class of civilization to another, and that the metals came gradually into use. The lake-dwellings were not burned down by the irruption of a foreign people; for at Niederwyl, and several settlements of the Unter-See, no traces of fire have been observed. The fact that but a very few human skeletons have been found in the whole settlements, contradicts the supposition of a battle having taken place between the aborigines and the supposed conquerors, and of the destruction of the former by the latter.[72]

Lake-dwellings belonging to this age and the bronze, have been found in Bavaria, Northern Italy, Mecklenburg, Pomerania, France, England, Scotland, and Ireland. Herodotus says that the Paeonians lived this way in Lake Prasias (Thrace), and Lubbock says that the fishermen of Lake Prasias still inhabit wooden huts built over the water. The town of Tcherkask in Russia, is constructed over the river Don, and Venice itself is but a lacustrine city.[73]

Several attempts have been made to estimate the time which has elapsed since the neolithic period. The estimates of M. Morlot are based on the discoveries made in a hillock formed by the river Tiniere at its entrance into the lake of Geneva. This cone contained three distinct layers of vegetable earth placed at different depths between the deposits of alluvium. The first was at a depth of three and one-half feet from the top, and was from four to six inches thick, and in it were found relics of the Roman period; the second was five and one-fourth feet lower, and six inches thick, in which were fragments of bronze; the third was at a depth of eighteen feet from the top, and varied in thickness from six to seven inches, and contained fragments of the stone age. History proves that the layer containing the Roman relics is from thirteen to eighteen centuries old. Since that epoch the cone has increased three and one-half feet, and if the increase was the same in previous ages, then the bed containing the bronze is from twenty-nine hundred to forty-two hundred years old, and the lowest layer, belonging to the stone age, is from four thousand seven hundred to ten thousand years old.

The calculation by M. Gillieron was made from the discoveries near the bridge of Thiele. About one thousand two hundred and thirty feet from the present shore is the old abbey of Saint Jean, built in the year 1100. There is a document which seems to show that the abbey was built on the edge of the lake. Then, in seven hundred and fifty years the lake retired one thousand two hundred and thirty feet. The distance of the present shore from the settlement of the bridge of Thiele is eleven thousand and seventy-two feet, and consequently the settlement is not less than six thousand seven hundred and fifty years old.

M. Figuier assigns to the lake-dwellings an antiquity of from six to seven thousand years before the Christian era.[74]

CHAPTER XI.

MAN OF THE NEOLITHIC.

From the human bones found in peat-bogs and tumuli, man is represented as having a narrow but round skull, with a projecting ridge above the eyebrows, showing he was round-headed, his eyebrows overhanging, small of stature though stout, and having a great resemblance to the Laplanders. In many respects the race was much superior to that of the preceding epoch. Man advanced rapidly in the arts, and made great progress in civilization. He had passed out of the barbarous, and might be called a semi-barbarian.

Habitations.--Man's habitation varied according to the locality. In the extreme south of France he continued for a considerable length of time to occupy the caves and rock-shelters; in Switzerland, the pile-buildings, and in Denmark he undoubtedly had rude huts placed close together and in proximity to the shell-heaps.

Clothing.--Clothing also varied according to locality. Where the wild animals were numerous their skins were used--there being no incentive to substitute other material. Coarse material made of fibrous plants had come into use. The lake-dwellers clothed themselves with this material, and completely protected their bodies. They also used sandals for their feet, as these have been found with the usual indications of usage.

Food.--Where wild animals could be obtained they were used, and the marrow of the long bones extracted. To this, fish and birds were added. In Denmark the principal food was the different species of the edible mollusk. In Switzerland a higher order and greater variety of food was used. The meat of the wild animals, birds, and fish was varied with bread made of barley and wheat, and fruit and berries. The meat was not only obtained from the wild animal, but they provided against the uncertainty of the chase by domesticating the boar, ox, sheep, and goat. The horse and dog were domesticated to assist in the chase, but sometimes served for food, probably during a famine.

If these people were cannibals, the evidence must rest solely on the human bones discovered at a dolmen near the village of Hammer, Denmark, which had been subjected to the action of fire. They were found together with some flint implements. But this evidence is not sufficient to lead to the conclusion that at the funeral banquets human flesh was used along with the roasted stag.

Arts and Manufactures.--The flint hatchets of the refuse-heaps are generally of an imperfect type; the long knives indicate a considerable amount of skill; the bodkins, spear-heads, and scrapers are but little improved. In the latter part of this epoch, the various kinds of implements, especially in Switzerland, attained to a surprising degree of perfection, in so much so, it is difficult to understand how this was achieved without the use of metal. They were made into various shapes, and with the design of pleasing the eye.

Besides the various types of implements common to the different countries, the tribes of Denmark manufactured a drilled hatchet, which is combined in various ways with the hammer. A specimen of this type is represented in Fig. 16, now in the Museum of Copenhagen. It is pierced with a round hole, in which the handle was fixed. The cutting edge describes an arc of a circle, and the other end is wrought into sharp angular edges.

New inventions were brought into use. Among them was a comb which, according to shape, might be compared to the dung-fork of the American stables. Ornaments for the body, made of various materials were fashioned. Pottery was still in a rough state, though gradually improving. The loom was invented, and various kinds of cloth were manufactured. Also out of the fibrous plants cordage was made, which again was fashioned into nets for fishing. Many canoes at various places have been found, showing that they were not only used for fishing but also for carrying cargoes. Workshops were established, and there the stone implements were made and polished; one of these shops was at Pressigny.

[Illustration: FIG. 16. DANISH AXE-HAMMER, DRILLED FOR HANDLE.]

Some idea may be had of the vast number of stone implements which occur, when it is considered that in the Museum of Copenhagen there are about twelve thousand, consisting of flint axes, wedges, broad, narrow, and hollow chisels; poniards, lance-heads, arrow-heads, flint flakes, and half-moon-shaped implements. In other collections in Denmark there are twenty thousand implements. The museum at Stockholm contains about sixteen thousand, and the Royal Irish Academy owns seven hundred flint-flakes, five hundred and twelve celts, more than four hundred arrow-heads, fifty spear-heads, seventy-five scrapers, and numerous other objects of stone, such as sling-stones, hammers, whetstones, grain-crushers, etc.[75] Some of these implements, however, may belong to other epochs.

War must have been carried on to a considerable extent, as fortified camps have been discovered in Belgium, at Furfooz, and other places. Their weapons were the axe, the arrow, the spear, and possibly the knife. These were wrought with great care.

Agriculture.--Man commenced to till the ground in this age, and thus laid the true foundation of civilization. He probably was forced to do it. The beasts of the forest were gradually decreasing. They had nourished him in the infancy of his mind, and now he should begin to look to the soil, and by the cultivation of its products he must sustain his life. His principal implement of agriculture must have been the sharpened stick, pointed with deer-horn. He cultivated the cereals, made his corn-mill, and stored the grain for winter use.

Burial.--How the colonists of the lake-dwellings disposed of their dead is unknown. In Denmark, and many other places, the dead were buried in dolmens or tumuli. A dolmen is a monument consisting of several perpendicular stones covered with a great block or slab. When it is surrounded by circles of stone it takes the name cromlech. The dolmens occur also in Scandinavia, France, and Brittany. They were formerly considered to have been Druidical sacrificial altars. They were usually covered over with earth, and in them were buried from one to twenty persons, accompanied with their implements. When a person died, the tomb was reopened to receive the new occupant. At such a time fire was used for the purpose of purifying the atmosphere of the tomb. In Brittany, in the vicinity of the tombs, there were set up in the ground enormous blocks of stone, that have received the name of menhirs, the most noted of which is that at Carnac. When these dolmens remain in the state in which they were left, still covered with earth, they take the name of tumuli. Comparatively few of the tumuli belong to the neolithic. In these, large numbers of bodies have been found, and none of them in a natural position, but cramped up and their heads resting between the knees.

Judging from the calcined bones, which are frequently met with at the tomb, it may be inferred that victims were offered during the funeral ceremonies, perchance a slave, or the widow. Lubbock is of opinion that when a woman died in giving birth to a child, or even while still suckling it, the child was interred alive with her.[76]

This hypothesis is substantiated by the great number of cases in which the skeleton of a woman and child have been found together. In the ceremonies at the tomb, some read the belief in a future state of existence. The evidence, however, is no clearer than that in the previous epochs. Man undoubtedly had such a belief, but science does not reveal it.

CHAPTER XII.

BRONZE EPOCH.

The Age of Bronze bears no direct relation to the antiquity of man, for it is largely embraced in written history. Although history does not record the events of the age of bronze in Western Europe, yet history covers the time which embraces the use of bronze. This epoch has more to do with the archaeologist than the geologist. It is marked by the abundance of swords, spears, fish-hooks, sickles, knives, ornaments, and other articles made of bronze. The bronze implements are principally found in England, Scotland, Ireland, France, Denmark, Norway, Italy, and Switzerland. The lake-settlements of Switzerland known to belong to this epoch are: Geneva, ten settlements; Neuchatel, twenty-five settlements; Bienne, ten settlements; Morat, three settlements; and Sempach, two settlements. To these may be added some of the crannoges of Ireland; also many tumuli and mounds.

Type.--The man of this epoch was not unlike that of the preceding. His head was rather broad than long, he was small, energetic, and muscular; his hands were small, as is proven by the remarkably small handles of their swords, which are too small for a hand of the present day. This type of man has maintained itself in the north of Switzerland to the present time.

Habitations and Food.--The caves and rock-shelters gave way entirely to the rude huts which now protected man. If they were resorted to, it was only from some peculiar cause or danger. The food was the same as in the neolithic, with additions to the cereals.

Clothing.--The skins of animals were used less than formerly for clothing. Garments made of other material have been found, and even the whole dress of a chief. In a tumulus of Jutland there were found a thick woollen cap, a coarse woollen cloak (Fig. 17), semicircular in form, scalloped out round the neck, shaggy in the inside, three feet four inches long, and wide in proportion; two woollen shawls, a woollen shirt, woollen leggings, and the remains of a pair of leather boots. Fibrous plants also contributed to the comfort of man, and were possibly used for summer wear, and under garments in winter.

[Illustration: FIG. 17. WOOLLEN CLOAK OF THE BRONZE EPOCH, FOUND IN 1861, IN A TUMULUS IN JUTLAND.]

Implements.--The people of this age made great improvements in their weapons, tools, and ornaments. They consist of bronze celts, swords, hammers, knives, hair-pins, small rings, ear-rings, bracelets, fish-hooks, awls, spiral-wires, lance-heads, arrow-heads, buttons, needles, various ornaments, saws, daggers, sickles, and double-pointed pins. There were also ornaments of gold. Only one implement, a winged celt, has been found, which bore an inscription.

Arts.--Progress was made in the art of weaving. Soldering and the moulding of metal were practised; foundries were established, the remains of which have been discovered at Devaine and Walflinger in Switzerland; stone moulds were used, one of which, on trial, produced a hatchet exactly similar to those which have been collected. The moulds were usually made out of sand. The crucible used for the melting of the metal was made out of pottery which was placed over a hole in the earth filled with burning charcoal; when the metal was melted, it was poured into the mould. Pottery took new shapes and was adorned with various patterns. Glass, which has so long been ascribed to Phoenician origin, was invented in the bronze age, for glass beads, of a blue or green color, have been found in the tombs of this epoch.

Agriculture.--The cereals attest to the tilling of the soil. The ground was prepared by the projecting branch of a stem of the tree, used as a plough. The grain was stored for winter use, and when required was crushed by being rubbed between two stones serving as a mortar.

Fishing and Navigation.--There are no distinct traces of improvement beyond the past epoch, in fishing and navigation, unless it be in the improved hooks made of bronze.

Burial.--The custom of burning the dead was almost universal in Denmark, and was more or less practised in other countries. The ashes and fragments of the bone were collected and placed either in or under an urn. When buried, the corpse was usually placed in a contracted position, but occasionally extended. With the dead were buried their implements and clothing. The body of the chief discovered in a tumulus in Jutland, where the clothing was found, was buried in a coffin nine and two-third feet long, over two feet in breadth, and covered by a movable lid. The body was in a good state of preservation, owing to the action on it of water strongly impregnated with iron. It was wrapped in the woollen cloak, and again wrapped in an ox's hide. Buried with it were the shawls, leggings, shirt, boots, and caps, two small boxes, a bronze razor, comb, a bronze sword in a wooden sheath, and a long woollen band. In other coffins have been found swords, knives, brooches, awls, tweezers, and buttons, all of bronze. In a baby's coffin was found an amber bead, and a small bronze bracelet.

Religious Belief.--Many crescents, made of stone and earthenware, have been found which are regarded, by some archaeologists, as religious emblems. Dr. Keller calls them "moon images," and has devoted a short chapter to their consideration.[77] On the other hand, Lubbock and Carl Vogt regard them as resting-places for the head at night.[78] They carefully arranged their long hair, and evidently sacrificed comfort for vanity. They carried a long pin with which to scratch the head. This kind of a pillow is still used by the Fuegeans and Abyssinians, who have their hair elaborately decorated; and in some cases this is never disturbed. If the people were worshippers the crescent is the only evidence from archaeology. No idols have ever been discovered. That the people were already worshippers may be learned from the traditions recorded in history.

CHAPTER XIII.

IRON EPOCH.

As the Iron Epoch fairly establishes civilization, and belongs almost wholly to the historical epoch, it will be here briefly noticed, and then dismissed after giving a quotation from Dr. Keller. The bronze had not only prepared the way for the iron epoch, but also gave a great impulse to succeeding ages. The art of metallurgy assumed a new importance and gave new life to every movement that tended to the assistance of man. The works of bronze gave way to those of iron. A knife made of iron is represented in Fig. 18. Knives of this pattern were, however, made of bronze, and served for the same purpose. The workshops of this age were so numerous that four hundred of them have been discovered in one province. The potter's wheel was invented; money was introduced, and agriculture greatly nourished.

[Illustration: FIG. 18. A KNIFE OF THE IRON EPOCH.]

Some of the Swiss lake-dwellings of Neuchatel and Bienne belong to this epoch. Dr. Keller, in summing up some of his observations, has made use of the following language: "The phenomenon of the lake-dwellings, so important in the history of civilization, the time of their first establishment, their original design, their development, and their final extinction, in spite of many accumulated facts, is in many respects clouded in doubt.... It is certain from the very beginning of this peculiar mode of living to the latest period of its existence, while outward circumstances remained the same, a quiet advance to a better development of the conditions of life may be observed, in which there was neither retrogression nor any sudden advance by the intervention of foreign elements. The general diffusion of metals in a country which had none, is explained simply by the barter which existed throughout Europe in the very earliest ages. The question why the inhabitants of a lake-dwelling of the stone age abandoned their settlements, while those of another, not many hours' or many minutes' walk distant, remained quietly living on their platforms, is of no greater importance than the inquiry why, during the middle ages, so many localities have disappeared, the names and situations of which are known to us. The presence of objects of industry on the area of the lake-dwellings has nothing in it very surprising, if we consider what misfortunes villages of straw-covered huts were exposed to, in which not only the houses themselves, but even the platforms on which they stood, were formed of very combustible materials. It is possible, if we are to take Caesar's account literally, that when the Helvetii, whose arrival in the country is neither mentioned in history nor shown by archaeology, withdrew, the lake-dwellings then existing were, as a whole, burned down; but there can also be no doubt that some remained standing, or were rebuilt after the return of the population. Their continuing down to the Roman time is only astonishing to any one who imagines that at this time the whole population had gone over to the Roman manner of life, while the proof lies before him that the lower class adhered to their own manners and customs till the entrance of the German races."[79]

CHAPTER XIV.

TRACES OF MAN IN AMERICA.

America furnishes a better field for the antiquary than the old world. Her ancient remains are not so much injured by the decay of empires and the rude hand of war. Succeeding ages have not so much effaced these marks, and many of the remains still stand as left by the original occupants, save only the change and decay which time itself produces. America will yet be discovered. It is true the landmarks are known; but these have not been investigated so diligently as the remains of man in Europe. The Boucher de Perthes and the Dr. Schmerling are yet to come. Until they do, the history of primitive man in America must be surrounded with great uncertainty. Much labor has been given to the investigation of this subject, and many works written, all looking toward an early development which must sooner or later come.

In this chapter the aim will only be to point out some of these traces.

Enumeration.--The implements from the gravel beds of Colorado and the skull from Calaveras county, California, have already been referred to (pp. 61, 62).

Near Osage Mission, Kansas, there was found a human skull imbedded in a solid rock, which was broken open by blasting. It was examined by Dr. Weirley, who compared it with a modern skull, and found it resembled the latter in general shape, yet it was an inch and a quarter longer. Of this relic he says: "It belonged to a man of a large size, and was imbedded in conglomerate rock of the tertiary class, and found several feet beneath the surface. Parts of the frontal, parietal, and occipital bones were carried away by the explosion. The piece of rock holding the remains weighs some forty or fifty pounds, with many impressions of marine shells, and through it runs a vein of quartz, or within the cranium crystallized organic matter, and by the aid of a microscope presents a beautiful appearance." In shape the Neanderthal man comes nearest to it.[80]

In the Comstock lode (Nevada), at a depth of five hundred feet, Judge A. W. Baldwin found a human skull of unusual and peculiar shape. It is very short from base to summit, and exceedingly broad between the ears. The skull is entire, with the exception of the facial bones. This skull has never been examined by a competent person.[81]

In the drift-clay, in the city of Toronto, at a depth of two feet from the surface, were discovered the bones and horn of a deer, amidst an accumulation of charcoal and ashes, and with them a rude stone chisel or hatchet.[82]

In the gravel of the gold-bearing quartz of the Grinell leads (Kansas), was found an imperfect flint knife at a depth of fourteen feet. Above the implement the gravel, composed of quartz and reddish clay, was ten feet thick, and above this was four feet of rich black soil. This implement was given to Dr. Daniel Wilson by Mr. P. A. Scott.[83]

Dr. Dickeson found, in the yellow loam of the Mississippi at Natchez, a human pelvic bone along with the bones of the mastodon and megalonyx. They were found at a depth of thirty feet from the surface, and the human bone had the same black color which characterized the others. Sir Charles Lyell calculated that it required sixty-seven thousand years to form the delta of the Mississippi, but admits, if the conclusions arrived at by the United States engineers be correct, in respect to the annual amount of sediment discharged at the delta, the growth would be reduced to thirty-three thousand five hundred years. Taking either of these estimates, the same would give the number of years which have elapsed since these bones were deposited.[84]

In an excavation made near New Orleans, at a depth of sixteen feet from the surface, beneath four cypress forests superimposed one upon the other, the workmen found a complete human skeleton, and some charcoal. The cranium is similar to the aboriginal type of the Indian race. This discovery furnished the data from which Dr. Bennet Dowler assigned to the human race an antiquity, in the delta of the Mississippi, of fifty-seven thousand years.[85]

Count Pourtalis found some fossil human remains, consisting of jaws, teeth, and some bones of the foot, in a calcareous conglomerate forming a part of the series of reefs of Florida. The whole series of reefs is of post-tertiary origin, and, according to Professor Agassiz, has been one hundred and thirty-five thousand years in forming. If this calculation be correct, then these bones must have an antiquity of ten thousand years.[86]

Dr. Lund, a Danish naturalist, explored eight hundred caverns in Brazil, belonging to different epochs, and exhumed in them a great number of unknown animal species. In a calcareous cave, near the lake of Semidouro, he found the bones of not less than thirty persons of different ages, and showing a similar state of decomposition to that of the bones of animals with which they were associated. From the discoveries there made, Lund was forced to the conclusion that man was cotemporaneous with the megatherium and the mylodon--animals belonging to the post-tertiary.[87]

The shell-heaps of America are coeval with those of Denmark. Those at Damariscotta, Maine, have been examined by Professor W. D. Gunning. He estimates that within, an area of one hundred rods in length, eighty in width there are piled one hundred million bushels of oyster shells. One dome-shaped hillock is nearly one hundred feet in height. The only human relics found among the shells are stone gouges, arrow-heads, bone needles, pottery, and copper knives. These shells were probably deposited by but a few individuals at a time. When formed, the oyster was a native of that coast, but within the memory of man the oyster has not lived there.

The Mound-Builders.--An ancient and unknown people of a certain degree of civilization have left remains of their greatness in the fortifications and mounds in the valleys of the Mississippi and its tributaries. These works extend over a great extent of territory. They are found in Western New York, West Virginia, Ohio, Kentucky, Tennessee, Indiana, Illinois, Wisconsin,

Michigan, Iowa, Nebraska, Missouri, Arkansas, Louisiana, Mississippi, Alabama, Georgia, Florida, Texas, and along the Kansas, Platte, and other western rivers.

The people appear to have originated in Ohio. On the southern extremity the works gradually lose their distinctive character, and pass into the higher developed architecture of Mexico; and at the north, north-east, and north-west, the population seem to have been more limited and their works less perfectly developed. The people were preeminently given to agriculture; were not warlike, and only navigated the rivers along their settlements. The fertile valleys of the Scioto, two Miamis, Kanawaha, White, Wabash, Kentucky, Cumberland, and Tennessee rivers were densely populated, as indicated by the numerous works which diversify their surfaces.

The stone and bone implements from the mounds, in their shape differ but little from those of Europe. The hatchets and knives are not only made of flint but also of obsidian, and other hard stones. Copper was the chief metallic substance. Out of this they made various implements, and swords. It was obtained from the shores of Lake Superior, where they carried on extensive mining. In these mines have been found their implements, some of which are very large diorite hatchets, used as sledges for breaking off lumps of copper, and so heavy that it would require more than one man to wield them. The copper was not subjected to heat, but it was hammered cold into such a shape as was desired.

Some idea of the number of the mounds and fortresses may be given from the statement that in the State of Ohio alone there are from eleven thousand to twelve thousand of these works. The fortresses were used for the protection of the people against the predatory warfare of the hostile tribes, or even, it may be, against the incursions made by other Mound-Builders. In regard to the mounds, there has been much speculation, and some archaeologists divide them into sacrificial, sepulchral, temple, and symbolical.

Sacrificial.--The sacrificial mounds are characterized by "their almost invariable occurrence within enclosures; their regular construction in uniform layers of gravel, earth, and sand, disposed alternately in strata conformable to the shape of the mound; and their covering a symmetrical altar of burned clay or stone, on which are deposited numerous relics, in all instances exhibiting traces, more or less abundant, of their having been exposed to the action of fire."[88] Among the most remarkable are those found on the Scioto, at the place called Mound City situated on the western bank. The mounds are enclosed by a simple embankment, between three and four feet high. The area occupied is about thirteen acres, and includes twenty-four mounds. One of these is one hundred and forty feet in length, and the greatest breadth is sixty feet. In this mound occurred four successive altars, a bushel of fragments of spear-heads, over fifty quartz arrow-heads, and copper and other relics. The sacrificial deposits do not disclose a miscellaneous assemblage of relics, for on one altar hundreds of sculptured pipes chiefly occur; on another, pottery, copper ornaments, stone implements; on others, calcined shells, burned bones; and on others, no deposit has been noticed. The sacrificial mounds are found at Marietta and other localities.

All the investigations which have been made prove that the altars were not only used for a long period, but also had been repeatedly renewed.

Sepulchral.--The sepulchral mounds are numbered by the thousands. They are simple earth-pyramids, sometimes elliptical or pear-shaped, and vary in height from six to eighty feet. Usually they contain but one skeleton, reduced almost to ashes, but occasionally in its ordinary condition and in a crouching position. By the side of them occur trinkets, and, in a few cases, weapons. These mounds were probably only raised over the body of a chief or some distinguished person.

Temple.--The temple mounds are truncated pyramids, with paths or steps leading to the summit, and sometimes with terraces at different heights. Among the most noted of these is that of Cahokia in Illinois. It is seven hundred feet long at its base, five hundred feet wide, and ninety feet high. Its level summit is several acres in extent.

Symbolical.--The symbolical mounds consist of gigantic bas-reliefs formed on the surface of the ground, representing men, animals, and inanimate objects. In Wisconsin they exist in thousands, and among the devices are man, the lizard, turtle, elk, buffalo, bear, fox, otter, raccoon, frog, bird, fish, cross, crescent, angle, straight-line, war-club, tobacco-pipe, and other familiar implements or weapons.

In Dane county there is a remarkable group, consisting of six quadrupeds, six parallelograms, one circular tumulus, one human figure, and a small circle. The quadrupeds are from one hundred to one hundred and twenty feet long, and the figure of the man measured one hundred and twenty-five feet in length and nearly one hundred and forty feet from the end of one arm to the other. Near the village of Pewaukee, when first discovered there were two lizards and seven tortoises. One of the latter measured four hundred and seventy feet.

In Adams county, Ohio, is the figure of a vast serpent; its head occupies the summit of a hill and in its distended jaws is a part of an oval-shaped mass of earth one hundred and sixty feet long, eighty wide, and four feet high. The body of the serpent extends round the hill for about eight hundred feet, forming graceful coils and undulations. Near Granville, Licking county, Ohio, on the summit of a hill two hundred feet high, is the representation of an alligator. Its extreme length is two hundred and fifty feet, average height four feet; the head, shoulders, and rump are elevated in parts to a height of six feet; the paws are forty feet long, the ends being broader than the links, as if the spread of the toes were originally indicated. Upon the inner side of the effigy is a raised space covered with stones which have been exposed to the action of fire; and from this leading to the top is a graded way ten feet in breadth. On examination it was discovered that the outline of the figure was composed of stones of considerable size, upon which the superstructure had been modelled in fine clay.

Antiquity.--There are methods of determining the antiquity of these mounds. Mr. E. G. Squier has pointed out three facts which go to prove that they belong to a distant period. 1. None of these ancient works occur on the lowest formed of the river terraces, which mark the subsidence of the streams. As these works are raised on all the others, it follows that the lowest terrace has been formed since the works were erected. The streams generally form four terraces, and the period marked by the lowest must be the longest because the excavating power of such streams grows less as the channels grow deeper. 2. The skeletons of the Mound-Builders are found in a condition of extreme decay. Only one or two skeletons have been recovered in a condition suitable for intelligent examination. The circumstances attending their burial were unusually favorable for preserving them. The earth around them has invariably been found wonderfully compact and dry; and yet, when exhumed, they have been in a decomposed and crumbling condition. 3. Their great age is shown by their relation to the primeval forests. As the Mound-Builders were a settled agricultural people, their enclosures and fields were cleared of trees, and remained so until deserted. When discovered by the Europeans these enclosures were covered by gigantic trees, some of them eight hundred years old. The trees which first made their appearance were not the regular forest trees. When the first trees that got possession of the soil had died away, they were supplanted, in many cases, by other kinds, till at last, after a great number of centuries, that remarkable diversity of species characteristic of North America would be established.[89]

Dr. Buchner assigns to them an antiquity of from seven thousand to ten thousand years.[90]

Fort Shelby, in Orleans county, New York, was carefully examined by Frank H. Cushing, the archaeologist. The fort was found to be composed of two parallel circular walls, with a gateway in each. The gateway in the outer wall fronted a peat-bog, the shore of which was some ten feet distant. Within the enclosure he found small, flat, notched stones, used for sinking fishing-nets. Into the bog he sank a shaft to the depth of seven feet, not far from the shore. At the bottom of the shaft he found the shells of living species of shell-fish. The natural surroundings show that this fort was built when the peat-bog was a lake. This is further confirmed by the fact that all ancient works are erected near a permanent supply of water. The nearest permanent supply of water is Oak Orchard Creek, one and one-half mile distant. The formation of this peat would require not less than four thousand years, and more probably twice that number.

The Mound-Builders must have remained a very long time. These works were formed gradually, and the population extended slowly toward the North. Their corn-fields, by their raised condition, show many successive years of usage.

NOTE A.--In reference to the fossil human bones from Florida Count L. F. Pourtales says: "The human jaw and other bones, found in Florida by myself in 1848, were not in a coral formation, but in a fresh-water sandstone on the shore of Lake Monroe, associated with fresh-water shells of species still living in the lake, (Paludina, Ampullaria, etc.) No date can be assigned to the formation of that deposit, at least from present observation."--American Naturalist, vol. II., p. 443.

NOTE B.--Besides the evidences already enumerated, Col. Charles Whittlesey gives the following: 1. Three skeletons of Indians in a shelter cave near Elyria, O., were found four feet below the surface, resting upon the original floor of the cave, upon which were also charcoal, ashes, and the remains of existing animals; estimated age, two thousand years. 2. Several human skeletons were found in a cave near Louisville, Ky., cemented into a breccia. They were discovered in constructing the reservoir in 1853. 3. A log, worn by the feet of man, was found in the muck bed at High Rock Spring, Saratoga, N. Y., at a depth of nine feet beneath the cave, and estimated by Dr. Henry McGuire to be 5,470 years old. It was discovered in 1866. 4. Mr. Koch claims to have found an arrow head fifteen feet below the skeleton of the Mastodon Ohioensis from the recent alluvium of the Pomme de Terre River, Mo., and now in the British Museum. His statement was, however, contradicted by one of the men who assisted him in exhuming the skeleton. 5. Dr. Holmes, of Charleston, S. C., found pottery at the base of a peat bog, on the banks of the Ashley River, in close connection with the remains of the Mastodon and Megatherium. 6. Col. Whittlesey, in 1838, found fire-hearths in the ancient alluvium of the Ohio, at Portsmouth, O., at a depth of twenty feet, and beneath the works of the Mound-Builders.--Col. Whittlesey before the American Association, in 1868.

CHAPTER XV.

WRITTEN HISTORY.

It is not generally known that written history extends so far back as to make worthless the present system of chronology. The mighty empires of antiquity must have been a mystery to many a thoughtful mind. As far back as history will carry us we not only behold the world teeming with her millions of people, but also nations rising and empires crumbling. Rollin felt the difficulties of the chronology which hampered him. He says the Assyrian empire was founded by Nimrod eighteen hundred years after the creation of man, or two hundred and twenty-four years after the Deluge, or one hundred and twenty-six years before the death of Noah. Nimrod was succeeded by his son Ninus, who received powerful succor from the Arabians, and extended his conquests from Egypt as far as India and Bactriana. Ninus enlarged his capital to sixty miles in circumference, built the walls to the height of one hundred feet, and so broad that three chariots could go abreast upon them with ease, and fortified and adorned them with one thousand five hundred towers two hundred feet high. After he had finished this prodigious work he led against the Bactrians one million seven hundred thousand foot, two hundred thousand horse, besides four hundred vessels well equipped and provided. After his death, Semiramis, his wife, ascended the throne. She enlarged her dominions by the conquest of a great part of Ethiopia. Then she led her army of three million foot and five hundred thousand horse, besides the camels and chariots of war, into India, where she suffered a severe defeat. After making these statements, Rollin says, "I must own I am somewhat puzzled with a difficulty which may be raised against the extraordinary things related of Ninus and Semiramis, as they do not seem to agree with the times so near the Deluge: I mean, such vast armies, such a numerous cavalry, so many chariots armed with scythes, and such immense treasures of gold and silver; ... and the magnificence of the buildings, ascribed to them."[91] The difficulties presented to the modern historian never would have occurred if discredit had not been thrown on the writings of the ancients.

Egypt.--The only history of Egypt, written in Greek, was that of Manetho, a high-priest of Heliopolis, who lived three hundred years before Christ. Only fragments of this work have been preserved. This history is taken from the ancient Egyptian chronicles, and records a list of thirty dynasties reigning in one city. His "thirty-one lists contain the names of one hundred and thirteen kings, who, according to them, reigned in Egypt during the space of four thousand four hundred and sixty-five years."[92] Dr. Buchner says Manetho "calculates for three hundred and seventy-five Pharaohs a reigning period of six thousand one hundred and seventeen years, which together with the present era, makes about eight thousand three hundred and thirty years."[93] Bayard Taylor makes Manetho assign the first dynasty to about the year 5000 B. C.[94]

Herodotus says the Egyptians "declare that from their first king (Menes) to this last mentioned monarch (Sethos), the priest of Vulcan, was a period of three hundred and forty-one generations; such, at least, they say, was the number both of their kings and of their high-priests, during this interval. Now three hundred generations of men make ten thousand years, three generations filling up the century; and the remaining forty-one generations make thirteen hundred and forty years. Thus the whole number of years is eleven thousand three hundred and forty." The priests "led me into the inner sanctuary, which is a spacious chamber, and showed me a multitude of colossal statues, in wood, which they counted up, and found to amount to the exact number they had said; the custom being for every high-priest during his life-time to set up his statue in the temple. As they showed me the figures and reckoned them up, they assured me that each was the son of the one preceding him; and this they repeated throughout the whole line, beginning with the representation of the priest last deceased, and continuing till they had completed the series."[95] From the time of Sethos, the priest of Vulcan, to the burning of the temple of Delphi, was one hundred and twenty-two years. The temple was burned B. C. 548. The period which, then, has elapsed from Sethos to the present (1875) is two thousand five hundred and forty-five years. Adding this to the time of Menes we have the whole period covering thirteen thousand eight hundred and eighty-five years. But if the generation be reduced to twenty years then the period from Menes to the present is nine thousand three hundred and sixty-five years.

The recent explorations made by Mariette among the archives of Egypt have confirmed the testimony of Manetho. The names of the kings, their order of succession, and the length of their reigns correspond with Manetho's table. These discoveries not only testify to the great antiquity of the empire, but also throw light on the nation, its manners, and customs. There were found stools, cane-bottomed chairs, work-boxes, nets, knives, needles, toilet ornaments, earthenware, seeds, eggs, bread, straw baskets, a child's plaything, paint boxes, with colors and brushes, etc., from three thousand to six thousand years old. There were also found the jewels of Queen Aah-hotep, who lived 1700 B. C., consisting of exquisite chains, diadems, ear-rings, and bracelets, which no modern queen would hesitate to wear.

These statements are still further confirmed by the testimony of geology. In the year 1850 borings were commenced in the mud deposit of the Nile. The most important results were obtained from an excavation and boring made near the base of the pedestal of the statue of Rameses at Memphis, the middle of whose reign, according to Lepsius, was 1361 B. C. Assuming with Mr. Horner that the lower part of the platform or foundation was fourteen and three-fourths inches below the surface of the ground, or alluvial flat, at the time it was laid, there had been formed between that period and the year A. D. 1850, or during the space of three thousand two hundred and eleven years, a deposit of nine feet four inches round the pedestal, which gives a mean increase of three and one-half inches in a hundred years. It was further ascertained, by sinking a shaft near the pedestal, and by boring in the same place, that below the level of the old plain the thickness of old Nile mud resting on desert sand amounted to thirty-two feet; and it was therefore inferred by Mr. Horner that the lowest layer (in which a fragment of burned brick was found) was more than thirteen thousand years old, or was deposited thirteen thousand four hundred and ninety-six years before the year 1850."[96] Other excavations were made on a large scale. In the first sixteen or twenty-four feet there were dug up jars, vases, pots, a small human figure in burnt clay, a copper knife, and other articles entire. When the water soaking through from the Nile hindered the progress of the workmen, boring was resorted to, and almost everywhere, and from all depths, even where they sank sixty feet below the surface, pieces of burned brick and pottery were extracted.[97]

Troy.--Troy, made immortal by the poem of Homer, has recently been uncovered to the eye of man, and fresh lustre has been thrown over the ancient bard. The descriptions of Troy given by Homer, thought to have been a mere work of imagination, are now shown to be accurate, and also that he must have been there. For the re-discovery and unearthing of Troy the world is indebted to Dr. Schlieman. Four buried cities superimposed one above the other were discovered. The third city, below the surface, is ancient Troy. The house of Priam, the Scaean gate, the massive walls and pavements, still remained. In the house of Priam Dr. Schlieman found a great mass of human bones, among them two entire skeletons wearing copper helmets, a silver vase, two diadems of golden scales, a golden coronet, fifty-six golden ear-rings, eight thousand seven hundred and fifty gold rings, buttons, etc. Immediately beside the house of Priam, closely packed in a quadrangular space, surrounded with ashes, and near by a copper key, were a large oval shield of copper, a copper pot, a copper tray, a golden flagon, weighing nearly a pound, several silver vases, a silver bowl, fourteen copper lance-heads, fourteen copper battle-axes, two large two-edged daggers, a part of a sword, and some smaller articles. The value, by weight alone, of all the gold and silver found in or near the house of Priam, has been estimated at twenty thousand dollars. During the excavations, over one hundred thousand articles were found. Every mark showed that Troy had been suddenly destroyed. Conflagration, ruin, the implements and the effects of war were visible. Even the brave warriors who fell while defending the palace of their king have not yet wholly crumbled into dust.

The four cities may be thus summed up: The topmost stratum is six and one-half feet in depth and covers the Grecian settlement which was established about the year 700 B. C. Beneath the Greek masonry are found the walls of another city, built of earth and small stones, but the abundance of wood-ashes shows that the city--or the successive cities--was chiefly built of wood.

The ruins of Troy, next in succession, are from twenty-three and one-half to thirty-three and one-half feet from the surface, and form a stratum averaging ten feet in thickness. Troy is supposed to have been founded about 1400 B. C., and its fall and destruction by fire to have occurred about 1100 B. C.

Under Troy there is a fourth stratum of ruins, varying from thirteen to twenty feet in depth. The most remarkable feature of these oldest ruins is the superiority of the terracotta articles. These vases are of a shining black, red, or brown color, with ornamental patterns, first cut into the pottery, and then filled with a white substance. The age of these ruins "is a matter of pure conjecture, since the vicissitudes of the city's history--frequent destruction and rebuilding--would have the same practical effect, or very nearly so, as a long interval of time. We have anywhere from two to five thousand years before Christ as the date of the foundation of the first Troy."[98]

Chaldea.--Berosus, a Chaldean priest of Belus, nearly three hundred years before Christ, wrote in Greek a regular history of Chaldea, in nine books. The materials for this work were supplied by the archives then existing in the Temple of Belus at Babylon. The work was particularly devoted to a history of the kingdom prior to the beginning of the Assyrian empire. Fragments of this work have been preserved by Josephus and Eusebius. After describing the cyclical ages of ten fabulous kings, he then comes to what he considers true history, and enumerates one hundred and sixty-three kings of Chaldea, who reigned successively from the time when the list begins to the rise of the Assyrian empire, about the year 1237 B. C. Berosus begins with a dynasty of eighty-six kings, and gives their names, which are now lost. He had no chronology of their time, but subjected it to a cyclical calculation. His list, which has so far escaped the lapse of time and the change of hands, is thus preserved:

First, eighty-six Chaldean kings; history and time mythical.

Second, eight Median kings; during two hundred and twenty-four years.

Third, eleven kings.

Fourth, forty-nine Chaldean kings.

Fifth, nine Arabian kings; during two hundred and forty-five years.

The rulers of the Assyrian empire were next added, as a sixth dynasty. The blank spaces in the list are doubtless the result of careless copying, or caused by imperfections in the manuscripts. In order to make the old kingdom of Chaldea begin about the year 2234 B. C. the first eighty-six kings of Berosus have been struck out as fabulous, and the Median dynasty regarded as spurious, and this without any show of reason, save that it does not agree with the chronology which the mutilators of history accept.

Investigations which have been made among the ruined cities of Chaldea have given great weight to the authority of Berosus, and are tending to the confirmation of his history. In Susiana there was found a Cushite inscription, mentioned by Rawlinson, in which there is a date that goes back nearly to the year 3200 B. C. The testimony of the records disentombed from the ruins, as well as Berosus, contradicts the prevalent hypothesis that the Magian or Aryan race occupied the country before the Cushites. These ruins also "confirm Berosus by showing that Chaldea was a cultivated and flourishing nation, governed by kings, long previous to the time when the city known to us as Babylon rose to eminence and became the seat of empire. During that long time there were several great political epochs in the history of the country, representing important dynastic changes, and several transfers of the seat of government from one city to another. Such epochs in Chaldean history are indicated by the list of Berosus."[99]

By this people, the science of astronomy was well understood. "Callisthenes, who accompanied Alexander to Babylon, sent to Aristotle from that capital a series of astronomical observations which he had found preserved there, extending back to a period of one thousand nine hundred and three years from Alexander's conquest of the city.... These observations were recorded in tablets of baked clay.... They must have extended, according to Simplicius, as far back as 2234 B. C., and would seem to have been commenced and carried on for many centuries by the primitive Chaldean people." A lens of considerable power, used for either magnifying or condensing the rays of the sun, was found at Babylon, in a chamber of the ruin called Nimroud.[100]

China.--Litse, an eminent Chinese historian, relates that there were long periods of time when the Chinese kingdom flourished, the chronology of which is not preserved, although there is recorded some knowledge of the rulers. One of these rulers promoted the study of astronomy. Next come the historical epochs. During the first, astronomy, religion, and the art of writing were cultivated. This was a great epoch, and ruled by fifteen successive kings. In the second epoch, agriculture and medical science were promoted. In the third, the magnetic needle was discovered, the written characters improved, civilized life advanced, and a great revolt suppressed. In the fourth and fifth epochs, the descendants of the previous ruler reigned. Next came the period of Yao and Shin. After this the period of the "Imperial Dynasties," which began with the Emperor Yu, who lived two thousand two hundred years B. C. The historical work of Sse-ma-thi-an narrates events chronologically from the year 2637 B. C. to 122 B. C.[101]

Mexico.--It is known that books or manuscripts were abundant among the ancient Mexicans. There were persons duly appointed to keep a chronicle of the passing events. Las Casas, who saw the books, says they gave the origin of the kingdom as well as the founders of the different cities, and every different thing which transpired that was worthy of note: such as the history of kings, their modes of election and succession; their labors, actions, wars, memorable deeds, good or bad; the heroes of other days, their triumphs and defeats. These chroniclers calculated the days, months, and years. Nearly all these books were destroyed at the instigation of the monks, and by the more ignorant and fanatical Spanish priests. A vast collection of these old writings were burned in one conflagration by order of Bishop Zumarraga. A few of the works, however, escaped, but none of the great books of annals described by Las Casas.[102] Thus Mexico must be left to the archaeologist unassisted by written history.

CHAPTER XVI.

LANGUAGE.

The origin and growth of language evidently afford a great field for study, in not only tracing the development of civilization, but also in confirming the testimony of the ancients and the conclusions of the geologists. If the unity of language could not be established, there would still be left a field so great as would not lessen the interest or the importance of the subject. But a new language cannot be formed. For the sake of convenience the many varieties of language have been grouped into three great divisions, i. e., the Aryan, the Semitic, and the Turanian. "The English, together with all the Teutonic languages of the Continent, Celtic, Slavonic, Greek, Latin with its modern offshoots, such as French and Italian, Persian, and Sanskrit, are so many varieties of one common type of speech: that Sanskrit, the ancient language of the Veda, is no more distinct from the Greek of Homer, ... or from the Anglo-Saxon of Alfred, than French is from Italian. All these languages together form one family, one whole, in which every member shares certain features in common with all the rest, and is at the same time distinguished from the rest by certain features peculiarly its own. The same applies to the Semitic family which comprises, as its most important members, the Hebrew of the Old Testament, the Arabic of the Koran, and the ancient languages on the monuments of Phoenicia and Carthage, of Babylon and Assyria. These languages, again, form a compact family, and differ entirely from the other family, which we called Aryan or Indo-European. The third group of languages, for we can hardly call it a family, comprises most of the remaining languages of Asia, and counts among its principal members the Tungusic, Mongolic, Turkic, Samoyedic, and Finnic, together with the languages of Siam, the Malay Islands, Thibet, and Southern India. Lastly, the Chinese language stands by itself as monosyllabic, the only remnant of the earliest formation of human speech."[103]

Anterior to these three families there was still another from which these were derived. It contained the germs of all the Turanian, as well as the Aryan and Semitic forms of speech. It belongs to that period in the history of man when ideas were first clothed in language, and has been called the Rhematic Period.[104]

As regards the origin of language, three theories have been proposed: the Interjectional, the Imitation, and the Root. The first supposes that the beginnings of human speech were the cries and sounds which are uttered when a human being is affected by fear, pain, or joy. The second supposes "that man, being as yet mute, heard the voices of birds, and dogs, and cows, the thunder of the clouds, the roaring of the sea, the rustling of the forest, the murmurs of the brook, and the whisper of the breeze. He tried to imitate these sounds, and finding his mimicking cries useful as signs of the objects from which they proceeded, he followed up the idea and elaborated language." The third theory, advanced by Max Mueller, is that language followed as the outward sign and realization of that inward faculty which is called the faculty of abstraction, and the roots, to which language may be reduced, express a general, not an individual idea.[105]

There is more or less truth in all these theories. At the very earliest period man must have possessed some method of communicating his wants or ideas. The casual observer has noticed that animals have methods of communicating with one another. It is not improbable that at the very earliest period man's only mode was that of cries and signs. This may have lasted for a very long time. Then the mimicking commenced. Next, comparison was resorted to when he had so far advanced as to describe his thoughts and, finally, from these various beginnings, from necessary or forced improvement, his ideas were expressed in root words.[106]

Instead of new languages originating, old languages change. They are mutable, and from them new dialects are produced. In the history of man there never has been a new language, and the languages now spoken are but the modifications of old ones. The words now used by all people, however broken up, crushed, or put together, are the same materials as were used in the beginnings of speech. New words are but old words; old in their material elements, though they may be renewed and dressed in various forms. "The modifiability of the language and its tendency to vary never cease, so that it would readily run into new dialects and modes of pronunciation if there were no communication with the mother country direct or indirect. In this respect its mutability will resemble that of species, and it can no more spring up independently in separate districts than species can, assuming that these last are all of derivative origin."[107]

There are from four thousand to six thousand living languages. The number of unspoken languages is not known. Their growth has required ages, and during their development many a parent stalk has ceased to exist. The changes in a language are slowly produced. It requires centuries to so far leave a language as to need an interpreter in order to understand it. Some idea of this slow change may be gained by comparing the writings in the English language of different periods. In the year 1362 appeared a poem called "Piers Ploughman's Creed," which begins as follows:

"In a summer season, When soft was the sun, I shoop me into shrowds[108] As I a sheep[109] were; In habit as an hermit Unholy of werkes, Went wide in this world Wonders to hear; Ac[110] on a May morwening On Malvern hills Me befel a ferly,[111] Of fairy me thought." Etc.

Written language is more permanent than spoken, but the process of either is necessarily slow. When it is remembered that a language has been derived successively through numerous others, no special limit or time can be given, although a very long period would be required. The usually accepted chronology would not allow sufficient time for the diversity in the Semitic family, to say nothing of the time required for the development of the three general classes.

CHAPTER XVII.

UNITY OF THE HUMAN RACE.

The theory of the unity of the human race has caused a clash of opinions among men of science. It has been the great battle field among anthropologists, ethnologists, geologists, philologists, and theologists. Men of acknowledged ability have been arrayed on either side. Among the foremost in favor of a diversity of origin have been Agassiz, Sir Roderick I. Murchison, Georges Pouchet, A. R. Wallace, and Schleicher. But the weight of evidence and authority is most in favor of the unity of the human race.

The advocates of the theory of the diversity of the origin of the human race have advanced many objections against the unity, and produced arguments in favor of their opinions. These may be summed up under five heads. 1. The anatomical differences between the different races, and especially those which distinguish the black and white. 2. The separation of the races from each other for unknown ages by great oceans, and by formidable and almost impassable continental barriers. 3. The disparity in intelligence, and the grades in civilization. 4. A medium type cannot exist by itself, except on the condition of being supported by the two creating types. 5. When two types become united, two phenomena may arise: a, Either one of them will absorb the other; or b, They may subsist simultaneously in the midst of a greater or less number of hybrids.

The following answers may be given to these objections, or arguments: 1. It is just as reasonable to suppose that man is affected, as well as the animals, by climate, food, or peculiar condition. It is well known that animals have undergone more or less change by their situation or position. Elephants and rhinoceroses are almost hairless. As certain extinct species, which formerly lived under an arctic climate, were covered with hair or long wool, it would appear that the present species of both genera had lost their hairy covering by exposure to heat. This is confirmed by the fact that the elephants of the elevated and cool districts of India are more hairy than those on the lowlands.[112] A wonderful change is wrought by the influence of climate on turkeys. In India "it is much degenerated in size, utterly incapable of rising on the wing, of a black color, and with long pendulous appendages over the beak, enormously developed." "In the English climate an individual Porto Santo rabbit recovered the proper color of its fur in less than four years."[113] Observers are convinced that a damp climate affects the growth of the hair of cattle. The mountain-breeds always differ from the lowland breeds; in a mountainous country the hind limbs would be affected from exercising them more, which would also affect the pelvis, and, then, from the law of homologous variation, the front limbs and head would probably be affected.[114] One of the most marked distinctions in the races of man is that the skull in some is elongated or dolichocephalic, and in others rounded or brachycephalic. Mr. Darwin has observed that a change takes place in the skulls of domestic rabbits; they become elongated, while those of the wild rabbit are rounded. He took two skulls of nearly equal breadth, the one from a wild and the other from a large domestic rabbit, the former was only 3.15, and the latter 4.3 inches in length. Welcker has observed "that short men incline more to brachycephaly and tall men to dolichocephaly; and tall men may be compared with the larger and longer-bodied rabbits, all of which have elongated skulls."[115] The argument from language is of great weight, especially in considering the differences in color. Professor Max Mueller has stated this clearly: "There was a time when the ancestors of the Celts, the Germans, the Slavonians, the Greeks and Italians, the Persians and Hindus, were living together beneath the same roof." "The evidence of language is irrefragable, and it is the only evidence worth listening to with regard to ante-historical periods. It would have been next to impossible to discover any traces of relationship between the swarthy natives of India and their conquerors, whether Alexander or Clive, but for the testimony borne by language."[116] When the great lapse of ages is taken into consideration, since man originated, it will be seen that sufficient time is given to produce the white, black, yellow, red, and brown varieties of man.

2. The argument from geographical distribution would hardly seem valid, as it is known that the ocean can be and has been navigated by frail crafts. Lieutenant Bligh, of the ship Bounty, in a small boat, twenty-three feet long from stem to stern, deep laden with nineteen men and one hundred and fifty pounds of bread, twenty-eight gallons of water, twenty pounds of pork, etc., started from the island of Tofoa (South Pacific) for the island of Timor, a distance of three thousand six hundred miles. In this voyage he encountered a boisterous sea, and great perils, but finally reached his destination.[117] When men began to dwell on the sea-coast they made their small vessels and carried on a limited navigation. Many a frail craft has been driven out to sea with its human freight, some of which landed on uninhabited islands. This has often happened among the South Sea islanders.[118] If it had been asserted, a few years ago, that man's distribution might have been partly caused by the agency of ice, it would have received no attention. And yet, Captain Tyson and his party, consisting of twelve men, two women, and five children, being a portion of the crew of the ill-fated Polaris, drifted about from the 15th of October, 1872, to the 30th of April, 1873, on an ice-floe, and in the midst of an arctic winter. Besides the provisions saved from the Polaris they subsisted on the flesh of seals, birds, and bears that they were able to kill. Every member of this party was rescued off the coast of Labrador. It must be further noticed that the surface of the earth was not always the same. The continents have changed more or less, and during these changes man must have become more or less separated.

3. In respect to the disparity it may be replied that the two extreme points

are observable in all the nations of the earth. Even in single families there have been those who were highly cultured and refined, while other members have been very low in organization, habits, and tastes. In these days it is manifest that all the races are capable of a very high degree of improvement. On the other hand, nations have retrograded. The ignorant, wretched nomads who pitch their tents amid the ruins of Babylon, are the descendants of the ancient mixed races who successively occupied Mesopotamia: the Assyrians, Babylonians, Medes, and Persians, who were ruled by such renowned monarchs as Shalmaneser, Nebuchadnezzar, Cyrus, and others. The wild marauding Arabs are the descendants of a people who invented algebra and introduced the numerals. So the list might be extended.

4 and 5. The fourth and fifth amount to the assumption that no race will amalgamate with another. The statements embraced under these two heads are not warranted by facts. Dr. Prichard says, "Mankind of all races and varieties are equally capable of propagating their offspring by intermarriages, and that such connections are equally prolific whether contracted between individuals of the same or of the most dissimilar varieties. If there is any difference, it is probably in favor of the latter."[119] He then gives a short account of several examples of new or intermediate stocks which have been produced and multiplied. They are Griquas, descended from the Dutch and Hottentots, who occupy the banks of the Orange River, and number five thousand souls; the Cafusos of Brazil, a mixture of native Americans and African Negroes; the Papuas of the island of New Guinea, a mixture between the Malays and Negroes. One of the best examples yet furnished is that of the Pitcairn Islanders. This colony originated in this way: The British government had sent a vessel, called the Bounty, commanded by Lieutenant Bligh, to gather bread-fruit trees at Otaheite and introduce them into the West Indies. Bligh was an overbearing, tyrannical, and cruel officer. Driven to fury, and out of patience with the superior officer, Mr. Fletcher Christian and others mutinied, and turned Bligh and his eighteen companions adrift. The mutineers proceeded to Tahiti; here they took on board provisions and live stock, nine Tahitian men, twelve women, and eight boys who had secreted themselves, and then proceeded to Toubouai, where they founded a settlement. Owing to dissensions the colony broke up and removed to Tahiti. But Mr. Christian, with eight other of the mutineers, three Toubouaians, three Tahitian men with their wives, and one child, and nine other women, left in the Bounty and landed at Pitcairn's Island, and there burned the

Bounty on the 23d of January, 1790. In less than nine years afterward, owing to strifes, the men were reduced to two in number, both whites, and one of them died the succeeding year. In the year 1808 the American ship Topaz touched at the island. The colonists then numbered thirty-five. In 1856 they had increased to the number of one hundred and ninety, and as the produce of the island was barely sufficient to support them they were removed by the British government to Norfolk Island. There are only eight surnames among them--five of the Bounty stock and three new-comers. They are a fine, healthy race of people; the men of a bright copper color, but the women are scarcely distinguishable from English women. If reports be true concerning them, they are the most remarkable people on earth. They never allow the sun to go down on their wrath, and are noted for their honesty, truth, chastity, industry, benevolence, reverence, simplicity, and all the virtues which combine to form true religion.

The law of hybridity, which has been so strongly urged against the unity of the race, has proved an argument in favor. The offspring of birds as much alike as the domestic goose and the large Muscovy duck will not propagate their species. Mules cannot perpetuate their kind. The different varieties of the horse, such as the little black Shetland pony and the tall white Arabian, will not only breed together but these hybrids will continue to perpetuate their kind, thereby proving their identity of species. The same may be said of the cross between the most perfect and the lowest type of mankind. If some of these mixtures die out in a few generations, it is not owing to their hybridity, but to the plain violation of natural laws. When the contracting parties to a marriage are of the same constitution, there will be no issue; if the constitutions, or rather, temperaments, are in substance too nearly the same, the issue, if any, will be either still-born, or die very soon after birth; if the contracting parties shall have an adjunctive element, the issue will be short-lived, although they may arrive at the years of maturity.[120] These laws apply to both the mixed and the unmixed types of mankind.

The close affinity of all the races, their subjection to the same general laws, their capacity for mental and moral improvement, and the virtual unity of their languages lead to the conclusion that one birth-place was common to all. If that place be Central Asia, or any other locality, it must have been long before traditional times, when the one tribe was broken up and nations formed.

Races change so slow that they seem to be stationary. On the ancient Egyptian monuments are representations of the Negro, having exactly the same features which characterize that race at the present time; and some of these paintings date as far back as 2000 B. C.

Then from the unity of the race and the persistency in type, an almost incredible length of time must be assigned to permit of the great disparity as exhibited by the different types of mankind.

CHAPTER XVIII.

THE BIBLE AND SCIENCE.

No book has caused so much controversy as the Bible. It has been made to answer for the folly of both its friends and foes. The fierce assaults made by the sceptic have been the legitimate result of the preposterous claims made by its ignorant but too zealous friends. The Bible makes no such claims for itself as have often been made for it. Its meaning has been perverted, sentences distorted, and words changed in order to suit the caprice of its advocates. If it were a living, speaking existence, it would certainly beg to be delivered from its friends. It has been made to conflict with the investigations of science, and those engaged in interpreting the laws of nature have been branded as infidels, although they may have devout and reverent spirits. The Bible is not and makes no pretensions of being a book of science. It is designed to be a book of religion, and a history of the ancient Jews, and its references to scientific questions are only incidental. If the references to science, or the account of Creation be radically wrong, its teachings on questions of morals and religion would not be thereby invalidated. The Christian, or the Jew, has nothing to fear from the results of scientific investigation. But there is a duty devolving on him, and that is to leave his fanciful interpretations and come to the true meaning of the Scriptures, and there learn how the words were understood by those to whom they were originally addressed. The meaning of words, as used in the nineteenth century, is not to be connected with their signification as used in the past. There is a great distance that divides the present from the times of the Hebrews, and their language and thoughts from the English language and modern thought. The ancient Hebrews were not given to scientific pursuits, and could have been but comparatively little advanced in civilization.

It is not the design here to enter upon an investigation of the points raised between the Scriptures and science, but to confine the inquiry to such questions as the previous chapters have demanded.

Creation.--The first and second chapters of Genesis not only teach that God is the Creator of heaven and earth, but also the order of succession is given. It is not stated that the world was created out of nothing. The word "bara," translated "created," has a variety of meanings. According to Gesenius it means to cut, to cut out, to carve, to form, to create, to produce, to beget, to bring forth, to feed, to eat, to grow fat, to fashion, to make.[121] The idea presented seems to be this: The author asserts that heaven and earth owe their origin to God. Then he goes back and explains the successive stages of creation. At the commencement of the work the earth was formless and void, or in a nebulous condition, and from this preexisting mass the worlds were evolved. When this mass was created, if ever, the author of Genesis does not state.

Six periods, or "days," are given for the formation of the earth. The use of the words "evening and morning" naturally leads to the conclusion that the days were each twenty-four hours in length. But doubt is thrown over this conclusion by the use of the word day in the second chapter and fourth verse, where the whole creative week is called a day. The word translated "day" also means time, but it is to be generally taken in the sense of the civil day--from sun up to sun down. Hugh Miller held to the opinion that the creation was represented to Moses in a vision. The periods passed before his mind in succession and had the appearance of days. The evening was the closing of one and the morning was the beginning of another period of time.[122] If a description of the different orders of life had been given, it would have been beyond the comprehension of that primitive people. It was not the design to teach geology. The people were not prepared for such scientific knowledge. But the simple statement that God is the author of all things, could be and was understood by the Israelites.

On the sixth day man appears; but there are two records, and in them he is presented in different ways and for different purposes. In the first account man is made in the image of God, and to him is given dominion over the living things, and he is commanded to subdue the earth. The second account states that there was no man to till the ground, and the Lord formed man of the dust of the ground, and breathed into his nostrils the breath of life; and man became a living soul. The second account cannot be, as has been assumed, a repetition of the first. The two accounts are radically different. One account makes man to have dominion over the beasts, birds, and fishes; the other, to till or cultivate the soil. This agrees with archaeo-geology. Men were hunters many ages before they were agriculturists. The one account has man made in the image of God, the other, a living soul. The "image of God" and "living soul" may be the same, but why the change? There may be a cause for it. If the theory of the vision be the true one, then Moses saw man in two capacities, differing one from the other. Man may be in the "image of God," and yet in a low, savage condition--subsisting on the chase. Man may be awakened from that condition, the "image of God" may assert its majesty, and make man a religious, worshipful being.[123] That there were two classes the record implies. Cain goes out into the Land of Nod, where his wife conceives, and he builds a city. Where did Cain get his wife, and why did he build a city? No account is given of the birth of his wife, but the natural inference is he obtained her in the Land of Nod.[124] It has been contended that Cain married his sister. If this be true it would certainly have been mentioned. It is too important a matter to have escaped notice. If he married his sister he was guilty of a heinous crime. If it was right then, it is right now. The city he built must have been more than an encampment, or a small fortification. (The word translated "city" bears this meaning also.) It would have been of no moment. It must have been a place of some consequence, and designed for more persons than Cain, his wife, and son. Taking all the circumstances together, including Cain's dread "of every one that findeth me shall slay me," it would seem that the object of this city was to provide for individuals of the pre-Adamic family dwelling on the east of Eden, and possibly to ingratiate himself into their favor.

Then, again, in the sixth chapter, "The sons of God saw the daughters of men that they were fair; and they took them wives of all which they chose." This was followed by great wickedness, in consequence of which the world was destroyed by a flood. Who were the "sons of God," and who the "daughters of men"? Why not the daughters of God? The "sons of God" must have been the lineal descendants of Adam, and the "daughters of men" the offspring of the pre-Adamic race. The mongrel race produced were monsters,[125] and their minds were bent continually on doing evil. These sons of Adam must have retrograded, or else they would not have sought wives from among a lower people. By the laws of nature their offspring was lower than either of the races, from the fact that to the brutish natures of the pre-Adamic type would be added the natural wisdom of the Adamic, thus producing cunning and craft in their wickedness.[126] If stringent moral laws had been enforced upon them the result would have been reversed.

Chronology.--The chronology given in the margins of the Bible is a mere invention, and has worked much mischief. There is nothing to warrant it, and no excuse can be made for it. The Bible gives no definite chronology for those early times. That no dependence can be placed in these chronologies is shown from the discrepancies between the Septuagint and the Hebrew texts.[127] The Septuagint dates the Flood eight hundred years farther back than the common Bible. "A margin of variation amounting to eight centuries between two versions of the same document, is a variation so enormous that it seems to cast complete doubt on the whole system of interpretation on which such computations of time are based."[128]

The Deluge.--Allowing the date of the Deluge to have been 3149 B. C. instead of 2349 B. C., still there is not sufficient time to repopulate the earth, and form those mighty empires recorded in ancient history. The Duke of Argyle has very justly remarked that, "The founding of a monarchy is not the beginning of a race. The people among whom such monarchies arose must have grown and gathered during many generations." The peopling of Egypt is not the only difficulty. "The existence, in the days of Abraham, of such an organized government as that of Chedorlaomer shows that two thousand years B. C. there nourished in Elam, beyond Mesopotamia, a nation which even now would be ranked among 'the Great Powers.'"[129] Then the characteristic features of the Negro, one of the most strongly marked among the varieties of man, were as greatly marked 2000 B. C. as at present.

These statements lead to the conclusion that the Flood was not universal. Most nations have a tradition of a flood, but "the monuments of the two most ancient civilizations of which we have any knowledge--the Egyptian and Chinese--contain no account of, or allusion to, Noah's Deluge."[130] Many of these traditions doubtless refer to some local flood. The passages of Scripture seem to teach the universality of the Deluge, but the same expressions which convey the idea of universality, are sometimes used in a limited sense, and refer only to the Holy Land, and to bordering regions. The question is one of doubt whether or not the sacred historian means the Noachian Deluge to have been universal, or only a local cataclysm.

Monarchies.--The Scriptures do not state that Nimrod was the first monarch, but "the beginning of his kingdom was Babel, and Erech, and Accad, and Calneh." Nor is the statement made that he founded these cities. He was a mighty hunter, and these cities were the beginning of his kingdom.

The Dispersion.--The building of the tower of Babel is no myth, but a veritable reality. A portion of the mighty fabric still stands, a mountain of ruins, attesting to the vast amount of work it required in its construction. The story is told in few words, and those words cover centuries. The people engaged in its construction spoke one language, but when this language was confounded the empire was rent asunder. The narrative seems to teach the use of but one language on the whole face of the earth. Dr. F. H. Hedge, in his sermon on "the Great Dispersion," says, "Moreover, the phrase 'the whole earth,' as commonly used in the Bible, is not to be taken in an absolute or scientific sense. It is not intended to include the entire globe, or even the greater part thereof, but is loosely employed to designate the whole of that particular portion which the writer or speaker has in his mind at the time. In the present case it denotes the country bordering on the Tigris and the Euphrates."[131] If the views of this eminent theologian be correct, then, by the same principle of interpretation the unity of language spoken of, is limited to the country bordering on the Tigris and the Euphrates.

There is no necessity of a supernatural aid for the origination of language. Under the view already advanced, when the animals were brought to Adam, he readily gave them names, for he had received language from his predecessors, and now, being an especially chosen person, his endowments would lead him to a more vigorous application of its use.

It is not incredible that God could have fashioned the world and peopled it with myriads of beings in a period of six days of twenty-four hours each. It is not incredible that a cataclysm could destroy every living creature, save an appointed few, and cover the remotest boundaries of the earth. It is possible for God to do anything save that which is inconsistent with his character.

What is possible for God to do, and what He does, are two very different things. What He has done can only be told from the evidences which He has left. What He might have done is only speculation. Man can only judge from the facts presented to him. He observes the course of nature, and from these observations his conclusions are drawn.

The world of nature and the spirit of revelation, when properly understood, are seen to be in harmony. Man is not to close his eyes and refuse to be guided by science, and with blind credulity accept the tales and prejudices of his grandfathers.

NOTE.--Dean Stanley, an eminent divine of the Church of England, in his discourse at the funeral of Sir Charles Lyell, takes unusual grounds for a theologian. He is reported as saying that there were and are two modes of reconciling the letter of Scripture with geology, but each has totally and deservedly failed. One of these attempts to wrest the words of the Bible from their real meaning, and force them to speak the language of science; the other attempts to falsify science to meet the supposed requirements of the Bible. But there is another reconciliation of a higher kind, or rather an acknowledgment of the affinity and identity which exist between the spirit of science and the spirit of the Bible. First, there is a likeness of the general spirit of the Bible truths; and, secondly, there is a likeness in the methods. The frame of this earth was gradually brought into its present condition by the slow and silent action of the same causes which we see now operating through a long succession of ages beyond the memory and imagination of man. We do not expect this doctrine to agree with the letter of the Bible. The early biblical records could not be literal, prosaic, matter-of-fact descriptions of the beginning of the world. It is now clear that the first and second chapters of Genesis contain two narratives of the Creation side by side, differing from each other in almost every particular of time and place and order. It is now known that the vast epochs demanded by scientific observation are incompatible both with the six thousand years of the Mosaic chronology and the six days of the Mosaic Creation. The discoveries of geology are found to fill up the old religious truths with a new life, and to derive from them in turn a hallowing glory.

GLOSSARY OF SCIENTIFIC AND DIFFICULT TERMS USED IN THIS VOLUME.

Adjunctive, having the quality of joining.

Alluvial, pertaining to the deposits of sand, clay, or gravel, made by river action.

Amalgamate, to mix or blend different things or races.

Antero-posterior, in a direction from behind forward.

Aphelion, that point of a planet's or comet's orbit which is most distant from the sun.

Archaeo-geologist, one versed in pre-historic remains, or familiar with both archaeology and geology.

Archives, public records and papers preserved as evidence of fact.

Aryan, a term applied to all the nations who speak languages derived mainly from the Sanskrit, or ancient Hindoo.

Atomic, a system of philosophy which accounted for the origin and formation of all things by assuming that atoms are endowed with gravity and motion.

Auditory, having the power of hearing.

Baton, a staff used as an emblem of authority.

Brachycephalic, a skull whose transverse diameter exceeds the antero-posterior diameter.

Breccia, a rock made up of angular fragments cemented together.

Bronze, an alloy of copper, with from ten to thirty per cent. of tin, to which other metals are sometimes added.

Calcareous, consisting of, or containing, carbonate of lime.

Calcined, reduced to a powder, or friable state, by the action of heat.

Carbonate, a salt formed by the union of carbonic acid with a base.

Carnivora, an order of animals which subsist on flesh.

Carpal, that portion of the skeleton pertaining to the wrist.

Cataclysm, a deluge.

Celt, one of an ancient race of people who formerly inhabited a great part of Central and Western Europe; an implement made of stone or metal, found in the ancient tumuli of Europe.

Cereal, edible grain.

Champlain Epoch, a name derived from the beds on the borders of Lake Champlain. The beds are subsequent in origin to the glacial epoch.

Chert, an impure variety of flint.

Clavicle, the collar-bone.

Conglomerate, rock made of pebbles cemented together.

Coronoid, the process of the ulna and lower jaw.

Cosmogony, the science of the origin of the world or universe.

Cranium, the skull.

Crannoges, small islets in the lakes of Ireland and Scotland, used by the ancients as places of habitation.

Crucible, a vessel capable of enduring great heat, and used for melting ores, metals, etc.

Cyclical, pertaining to a periodical space of time marked by the recurrence of something peculiar.

Data (pl. of datum), a ground of inference or deduction.

Debris (d[=a]-bree), fragments detached from rocks, and piled up in masses.

Demi-relief, the projection of one half the figure beyond the plane from which it rises.

Dendrites, a stone on which are tree-like markings.

Devonian, the geological age between the Silurian and Carboniferous.

Diluvium, the time when the glacial beds were deposited.

Diorite, a tough rock, in color whitish, speckled with black, or greenish black.

Dolichocephalic, a skull whose diameter from the frontal to the occipital bone exceeds the transverse diameter.

Dorsal, the name given to the second division of the vertebrae.

Drift, a collection of loose earth and bowlders, distributed during the glacial epoch over large portions of the earth's surface.

Druidical, pertaining to the religious ceremonies of the ancient Celtic nations in France, Britain, and Germany.

Dynasty, a succession of kings of the same line or family.

Eccentricity, the distance of the centre of the orbit of a heavenly body from the centre of the body round which it revolves.

Edible, eatable.

Elliptical, having an oval or oblong figure.

Eocene, the oldest of the three epochs of the tertiary.

Epoch, any period of time marked by some particular cause or event.

Esplanade, a clear space, or grass plat.

Fauna, the animals of any given area or epoch.

Flora, the complete system of vegetable species native in a given locality, or period.

Fluor-spar, a mineral of beautiful colors, composed by fluorine and calcium.

Fluvio-marine, the deposits formed by the joint action of a river and the sea.

Foramen, a little opening.

Fossa, a depression in a bone.

Fossil, the form of a plant or animal in the strata composing the surface of the earth.

Genus (pl. genera), an assemblage of species possessing certain characters in common, by which they are distinguished from all others.

Geode, an irregular shaped stone, containing a small cavity.

Geognostic, pertaining to a knowledge of the structure of the earth.

Glabella, the middle or frontal protuberance of the superciliary arch.

Glaciation, the process of becoming covered with glaciers.

Glacier, an immense mass of ice, or snow and ice, formed in the region of perpetual snow, and moving slowly down mountain slopes or valleys.

Gneiss, a crystalline rock, consisting of quartz, feldspar, and mica.

Herbivora, that order of animals which subsists upon herbs or vegetables.

Homologous, having the same typical structure.

Humerus, the bone of the arm nearest the shoulder.

Hybrid, that which is produced from the mixture of two species.

Ilium, the upper part of the hip bone.

Jade, a hard and compact stone, of a dark green color, and capable of a fine polish.

Lambdoidal, the suture which connects the occipital with the parietal bones.

Leptinite, a fine-grained granitic rock.

Loam, a soil composed of siliceous sand, clay, carbonate of lime, oxide of iron, magnesia, and various salts, and also decayed vegetable and animal matter.

Loess, a term usually applied to a tertiary deposit on the banks of the Rhine.

Lumbar, the vertebrae near the loins.

Mammalia, that class of animals characterized by the female suckling its young.

Marl, a mixed earthy substance, consisting of carbonate of lime, clay, and siliceous sand.

Mastoid, a process situated at the posterior part of the temporal bone.

Matrix, a mould; the cavity in which a thing is held.

Maxillary, the upper jaw bone.

Metacarpal, the part of the hand between the wrist and the fingers.

Metallurgy, the art of working metals.

Metatarsal, the middle part of the foot.

Miocene, the middle or second epoch of the Tertiary.

Molar, a grinding tooth.

Mold, or mould, a prepared cavity used in casting; to form or shape; fine soft earth.

Mollusca, an order of invertebrate animals having a soft, fleshy body, which is inarticulate, and not radiate internally.

Moraine, a line of blocks and gravel extending along the sides of separate glaciers, and along the middle part of glaciers formed by the union of one or more separate ones.

Nebulous, having a faint, misty appearance; applied to uncondensed gaseous matter.

Neolithic, new stone age; a term applied to the more modern age of stone.

Nummulitic, composed of, or containing a fossil of a flattened form, resembling a small coin, and common in the early tertiary period.

Obsidian, a kind of glass produced by volcanoes.

Occipital, pertaining to the back part of the head.

Ochreous, consisting of fine clay, containing iron.

Olecranon, the large process at the extremity of the larger bone of the fore-arm.

Onusprobandi, the burden of proof.

Orbit, the cavity in which the eye is located; the path described by a heavenly body in its periodical revolution.

Osar, a low ridge of stone or gravel formed by glaciers.

Oscillation, the act of moving backward and forward.

Osseous, composed of bone.

Osteologist, one versed in the nature, arrangement, and uses of the bones.

Oxide, a compound of oxygen, and a base destitute of acid and saltish properties.

Pachyderm, a non-ruminant animal, characterized by the thickness of its skin.

Palaeolithic, the ancient stone age; a term applied to the earliest traces of man when he was cotemporary with many extinct mammalia.

Palaeontological, belonging to the science of the ancient life of the earth.

Parallelogram, a figure having four sides, the opposite sides of which are parallel, and consequently equal.

Parietal, pertaining to the bones which form the sides and upper part of the skull.

Pathological, pertaining to the knowledge of disease.

Pelvic, pertaining to the open, bony structure at the lower extremity of the body.

Perihelion, that point in the orbit of a planet, or comet, in which it is nearest to the sun.

Perimeter, the outer boundary of a body.

Phalanges, the small bones of the fingers and toes.

Philologist, one versed in the laws of human speech.

Pliocene, a term applied to the most recent tertiary deposits.

Post-Tertiary, the second period of the age of mammals.

Prototype, a model after which anything is to be copied.

Quadrangular, having four angles, and consequently four sides.

Quadrumana, an order of animals whose fore feet correspond to the hands of man.

Quartz, a stone of great hardness, with a glassy lustre, and varying in color from white, or colorless, to black.

Quartzite, granular quartz.

Quaternary, same as Post-Tertiary.

Radius, the smaller and exterior bone of the fore-arm.

Reliquiae, remains of the dead.

Rhematic, that period when men first began to coin expressions for the most necessary ideas.

Rodent, an animal that gnaws.

Ruminant, an animal that chews the cud.

Sagittal, the suture which connects the parietal bones of the skull.

Savant (sae-v[)o]ng), a person eminent for acquirements.

Scapula, the shoulder-blade.

Schist, a rock having a slaty structure.

Scientist, a person noted for his profound knowledge.

Sediment, the matter which subsides to the bottom.

Semitic, pertaining to one of the families of nations, or languages, and so named from its members being ranked as the descendants of Shem.

Serpentine, a soft, massive stone, in color dark to light green.

Siliceous, containing silica, or flinty matter.

Simian, a name given to the various tribes of monkeys.

Squamous, the anterior and upper part of the temporal bone, scale-like in form.

Stalagmite, a deposit of earthy matter, made by calcareous water dropping on the floors of caverns.

Stratified, formed or deposited in layers.

Stratum (pl. strata), a bed or layer.

Subsidence, the act of sinking or gradually descending.

Superciliary, the bony superior arch above the eye-brow.

Suture, the seam which unites the bones of the skull.

Symphysis, a connection of bones without a movable joint.

Talus, a sloping heap of fragments of rocks lying at the foot of a hill.

Tarsal, relating to the ankle.

Temporal, pertaining to that portion of the head located to the front and a little above the ear.

Terra-cotta, a kind of pottery made from fine clay, hardened by heat.

Tertiary, the first period of the age of mammals.

Thoracic, pertaining to the breast or chest.

Troglodyte, an inhabitant of a cave.

Truncated, cut off.

Tufaceous, consisting of, of resembling, tuff.

Tuff, a sand rock formed by agglutinated volcanic rock.

Turanian, that order of languages known as monosyllabic.

Ulna, the larger of the two bones of the fore-arm.

Veda, the ancient sacred literature of the Hindoos.

Vertebra, a joint of the back bone.

INDEX.

Zawisza, Count, 88. Zumarraga, Bishop, 131.

FOOTNOTES

[1] "Pre-Historic Times," p. 2.

[2] Buchner, p. 269.

[3] "Man in the Past, Present, and Future," p. 238.

[4] "Antiquity of Man," p. 68.

[5] Discoveries of this kind were made in 1829.--Keller's "Lake-Dwellings," p. 11.

[6] "Principles of Geology," vol. i. p. 286.

[7] "Pre-Historic Times," p. 418.

[8] "Manual of Geology," p. 590.

[9] "Antiquity of Man," pp. 282, 285.

[10] "Pre-Historic Times," p. 417.

[11] Principles of Geology, vol. i. p. 285; "Pre-Historic Times," p. 411.

Mr. Croll believes that, owing to variations in the eccentricity of the earth's orbit "cold periods regularly recur every ten or fifteen thousand years; but that at much longer intervals the cold, owing to certain contingencies, is extremely severe, and lasts for a great length of time; and the last great glacial period occurred about two hundred and forty thousand years ago, and endured with slight alterations of climate for about one hundred and sixty thousand years."--Darwin's Origin of Species, p. 343.

[12] It would be plausible to assume that the ice melted much more rapidly than is generally supposed. Charles Darwin, in his "Naturalist's Voyage around

the World," p. 245, states that "during one very dry and long summer, all the snow disappeared from Aconcagua, although it attains the prodigious height of twenty-three thousand feet. It is probable that much of the snow at these great heights is evaporated, rather than thawed."

[13] "Principles of Geology," vol. ii, pp. 567-569.

[14] Buchner, p. 118

[15] "Pre-Historic Times," p. 362.

[16] "Antiquity of Man," p. 97; "Pre-Historic Times," p. 315.

[17] The "Science Record" for 1874, p. 501, in speaking of these implements says, "At the very lowest estimate, the flint weapons were made half a million years ago."

[18] "Antiquity of Man," p. 98. "Pre-Historic Times," p. 317.

[19] "Antiquity of Man," p. 338; Buchner, 27.

[20] "Antiquity of Man," p. 510; Buchner, p. 27.

[21] Buchner, pp. 118, 306.

[22] Buchner, p. 239.

[23] "Principles," vol. ii, p. 566.

[24] "Antiquity of Man," p. 63.

[25] It has been estimated by the British Association that it requires twenty thousand years to produce a foot of stalagmite.--Science Record. 1874, p. 601.

[26] "Principles," vol. ii, p. 527.

[27] "Man's Place in Nature," p. 146.

[28] "Pre-Historic Times," p. 337.

[29] "Antiquity of Man," p. 80.

[30] "Man's Place in Nature," p. 143.

[31] "Antiquity of Man," p. 80.

[32] Buchner, p. 263.

[33] Ibid. p. 262.

[34] "Man's Place in Nature," p. 158.

[35] Buchner, p. 241.

[36] Buchner, p. 240.

[37] Ibid. p. 241.

[38] "Man's Place in Nature," p. 164.

[39] Buchner, p. 116.

[40] "Antiquity of Man," p. 84.

[41] Ibid., p. 53.

[42] "Antiquity of Man," p. 84.

[43] Buchner, p. 54.

[44] Buchner, p. 242.

[45] Denton's "Our Planet," p. 270.

[46] Buchner, p. 265.

[47] Ibid., p. 54.

[48] Ibid., p. 242.

[49] "Pre-Historic Times," p. 422.

[50] Ibid., p. 423.

[51] Wallace's "Natural Selection, p. 322."

[52] Buchner, pp. 34, 252.

[53] Buchner, p. 242.

[54] Buchner, p. 31; "Pre-Historic Times," p. 420.

[55] Buchner, p. 33; "Pre-Historic Times," p. 421.

[56] Denton's "Our Planet," p. 270; "American Phrenological Journal, Feb." 1874.

Having seen the statement in one of the newspapers that this skull was not genuine, but a joke played on Professor Whitney, I wrote to Professor W. Denton of Wellesley, Masschussetts, on 19th March 1875, inquiring about it. A few days later I received from him the statement that he had visited the place where the skull was found; that certain persons assured him that Professor Whitney had been the victim of a joke. Yet these persons had never seen the skull, and were prejudiced against Professor Whitney. The persons who were best informed had every reason to believe the statements made by Professor Whitney were true. The skull is a very remarkable one, and stands alone for the enormous size of the orbits, and I have good reasons to believe it to have been found as stated.

[57] "Several geologists are convinced, from direct evidence, that glacial periods occurred during the miocene and eocene formations, not to mention still more ancient formations."--Darwin's Origin of Species, p. 343.

[58] "Pre-Historic Times," p. 421; Buchner, 32.

[59] "Pre-Historic Times," p. 422.

[60] Buchner, p. 32.

[61] "American Phrenological Journal," Feb. 1874.

[62] Buchner, p. 274.

[63] "Our Planet," p. 266.

[64] "Science Record," 1874, p. 499.

[65] "Pre-Historic Times," p. 315.

[66] "Origin of Civilization," p. 121.

[67] Figuier's "Primitive Man," p. 116.

[68] Buchner, p. 248.

[69] Buchner, p. 247; "Keller's Lake-Dwellings."

[70] "Lake-Dwellings," pp. 37, 334, 350, 360.

[71] "Lake-Dwellings," p. 394.

[72] "Lake-Dwellings," p. 396.

[73] "Primitive Man," p. 219.

[74] "Primitive Man," p. 293.

[75] "Pre-Historic Times," p. 76.

[76] "Primitive Man," p. 200.

[77] "Lake Dwellings," p. 319.

[78] "Pre-Historic Times," p. 218; "Primitive Man," p. 281.

[79] "Lake-Dwellings," p. 400.

[80] "Science Record," p. 564. 1875.

[81] "American Phrenological Journal," February, 1874.

[82] Wilson's "Pre-Historic Man," p. 40.

[83] "Pre-Historic Man," p. 46.

[84] "Antiquity of Man," p. 200; "Principles of Geology," vol. i. p. 454.

[85] "Antiquity of Man," p. 43; "Pre-Historic Man," p. 47.

[86] "Antiquity of Man," p. 44.

[87] "Primitive Man," pp. 9, 77.

[88] "Pre-Historic Man," p. 236.

[89] "Ancient Monuments," p. 304.

[90] Buchner, p. 35.

[91] Rollin, vol. i. p. 138.

[92] Anthon's Classical Dictionary, p. 788.

[93] Buchner, 254.

[94] "New York Tribune", June 6, 1874.

[95] Rawlinson's Herodotus, vol. ii. p. 189.

[96] "Principles of Geology," vol. i. p. 432.

[97] "Antiquity of Man," p. 36.

[98] Bayard Taylor in "New York Tribune, Extra," No. 15.

[99] "Pre-Historic Nations," p. 190.

[100] Ibid. pp. 178, 175.

[101] "Pre-Historic Nations," p. 37.

[102] "Ancient America," p. 187.

[103] "Chips from a German Workshop," vol. i. p. 21.

[104] Ibid. vol. ii. p. 8.

[105] Wake's "Chapters on Man," p. 33.

[106] "Diodorus Siculus, Lucretius, Horace, and many other Greek and Roman writers, consider language as one of the arts invented by man. The first men, say they, lived for some time in woods and caves, after the manner of beasts, uttering only confused and indistinct noises, till, associating for mutual assistance, they came by degrees to use articulate sounds mutually agreed upon, for the arbitrary signs or marks of those ideas in the mind of the speaker which he wanted to communicate to the hearer. This opinion sprung from the atomic cosmogony which was framed by Mochus, the Phoenician, and afterward improved by Democritus and Epicurus."--Pouchet's Plurality of the Human Race, p. 142.

[107] "Principles of Geology," vol. ii. p. 475. "It is generally acknowledged that all organic beings have been formed on two great laws--Unity of Type, and the Conditions of Existence. By unity of type is meant that fundamental agreement in structure which we see in organic beings of the same class, and which is quite independent of their habits of life. On my theory, unity of type is explained by unity of descent."--Darwin's Origin of Species, p. 200.

[108] I put myself into clothes.

[109] Shepherd.

[110] And.

[111] Wonder.

[112] "Descent of Man," vol. i. p. 143.

[113] Mivart's "Genesis of Species," p. 114.

[114] "Origin of Species," p. 193.

[115] "Descent of Man," vol. i. p. 142.

[116] "Chips," vol. i. pp. 63, 62.

[117] Lady Belcher's "Mutineers of the Bounty," p. 61.

[118] "Captain Cook found on the island of Wateoo, three inhabitants of Otaheite, who had been drifted thither in a canoe, although the distance between the two isles is five hundred and fifty miles. In 1696, two canoes, containing thirty persons, who had left Ancorso, were thrown by contrary winds and storms on the Island of Samar, one of the Philippines, at a distance of eight hundred miles. In 1721, two canoes, one of which contained twenty-four, and the other six persons, men, women, and children, were drifted from an island called Farroilep to the island of Guaham, one of the Marians, a distance of two hundred miles." Kadu, a native of Ulea, and three of his countrymen, while sailing in a boat, were driven out to sea by a violent storm, and drifted about the sea for eight months, subsisting entirely on the produce of the sea, and finally were picked up in an insensible condition by the inhabitants of Aur (Caroline Isles) one thousand five hundred miles distant from his native isle.--Principles of Geology, vol. ii. p. 472.

[119] "Natural History of Man," vol. i. p. 16.

[120] Powell's "Human Temperaments," p. 180.

[121] The idea that "bara" meant to create out of nothing is a modern invention, and most likely called forth by the contact between Jews and Greeks at Alexandria. The Greeks believed that matter was co-eternal with the Creator, and it was probably in contradistinction to this notion that the Jews first asserted that God made all things out of nothing. The word, however, only calls forth the simple conception of fashioning or arranging.-- Chips, vol. i. p. 132.

[122] "Testimony of the Rocks," Fifth Lecture.

[123] Rev. Dr. J. P. Thompson represents Adam as a typical man (Man in Genesis and Geology, p. 105); Lubbock regards him as a typical savage (Origin Civilization, p. 361). Why not call him the first great prototype of the human race?

[124] The word Nod means to wander, to be driven about, etc. It appears to have been a familiar name at the time of the fratricide. It was then the name of a land or tract of country. May there not have been roving tribes there, and from them the place was designated "Wandering Land"?

[125] Dr. Livingstone, after speaking of a half-caste man on the Zambesi, described by the Portuguese as a rare monster of humanity, "remarks, 'It is unaccountable why half-castes, such as he, are so much more cruel than the Portuguese, but such is undoubtedly the case.' An inhabitant remarked to Livingstone, 'God made white men, and God made black men, but the devil made half castes.' When two races, both low in the scale, are crossed, the progeny seem to be eminently bad. Thus the noble-hearted Humboldt speaks in strong terms of the bad and savage disposition of Zambos, or half-castes between Indians and Negroes; and this conclusion has been arrived at by various observers. From these facts we may perhaps infer that the degraded state of so many half-castes is in part due to reversion to a primitive and savage condition, as well as to the unfavorable moral conditions under which they generally exist."--Animals and Plants under Domestication, vol. ii. p. 63.

[126] This view does not conflict with the doctrine of the unity of the race. The great difficulty in interpreting the Scriptures is its briefness. A long period of time is comprehended in a very few words, and much is left to inference. The tenor of the Scriptures favors the idea of the unity of the race, still it is

not specifically declared. The strongest passage is Acts chapter 17 and verse 26: "Hath made of one blood all nations of men for to dwell on all the face of the earth." This does not conflict with the idea of there being more than one pair, but their blood is the same. It is not declared that Adam had no ancestors. When it is declared that Adam was the son of God, it is only to trace man's origin to the Supreme Being. If Adam had ancestors, the leaving of them out has no signification, as it was not uncommon to drop the name of unimportant persons. An instance of this kind is given in the genealogy of David. From the birth of Obed to the birth of his grandson David (common chronology) is a period of two hundred and twenty-three years. Evidently one or more members have been dropped. If Adam was a prototype it was not necessary to trace the line any farther back. The forming him of the dust of the ground would give his relationship to the rest of mankind. He was chosen, endowed for the purpose of elevating the race--of becoming the head of a new type of humanity.

[127] The Septuagint version is a translation of the Hebrew Bible into Greek, made about three hundred years B. C. The oldest existing MS. of the Old Testament in Hebrew dates back no farther than about the tenth century after the Christian era--Chips. vol. i. p. 11.

[128] "Primeval Man," p. 86.

[129] "Primeval Man," p. 87.

[130] "Primeval World of Hebrew Tradition," p. 195.

[131] "Primeval World of Hebrew Tradition," p. 222.